GENTLEMEN
ROGUES
& WICKED
LADIES

GENTLEMEN ROGUES & *WICKED LADIES*

A GUIDE TO BRITISH HIGHWAYMEN & HIGHWAYWOMEN

FIONA MCDONALD

To Carl, my very own Knight of the Road
and to Isabel Atherton whose brilliant idea it was

First published 2012

The History Press
The Mill, Brimscombe Port
Stroud, Gloucestershire, GL5 2QG
www.thehistorypress.co.uk

British Library Cataloguing in Publication Data.
A catalogue record for this book is available from the British Library.

ISBN 978 0 7524 6376 6

Typesetting and origination by The History Press
Printed in India

CONTENTS

AUTHOR'S NOTE

ACKNOWLEDGEMENTS

Thanks to my agent, Isabel Atherton of Creative Authors; my ever-supportive family for hearing endless talk about highwaymen and highwaywomen; Beatriz Alvarez for her keen proofreading and editing skills; Hayley Sherman for her edit; and of course a big thank you to the team at The History Press.

PRIMARY SOURCES

In researching this book I used a number of exceptional sources. The foremost of these was *The Newgate Calendar*. Lives and crimes of the inmates of Newgate prison were recorded by the ordinary of Newgate. Sometimes, the histories were told by the prisoners themselves to the ordinary. Other times, quite a bit of fiction slipped into them. One or two highwaymen left their memoirs in the hands of the ordinary who was to have them published after the authors' deaths. The ordinary was able to make a nice little earner on the side by taking down and publishing the lives and crimes of the criminals waiting to be hanged at Newgate.

The collection of accounts is vast and parts of it have been published in book form over two centuries and sold to a public avid for sensational and gory crime stories. It was common in the nineteenth century to give this type of book to children in an attempt to scare them away from becoming criminals themselves. The style of writing tended to be ponderous and a lot of the accounts were very similar. But, on the whole, *The Newgate Calendar* is a fascinating insight into the life of a criminal sentenced to hang.

Other important sources are the proceedings from the Old Bailey (these are transcripts of the trials themselves taken down during court) and leaflets published around the time of a sensational crime or execution. Thomas Kyll wrote *The Trial of the Notorious Highwayman Richard Turpin* and Richard Bayes, who was the innkeeper involved in the capture of the highwayman, wrote down his experiences as well as Turpin's in *The Genuine History of the Life of Richard Turpin*, 1739. There are discrepancies between Bayes's and Kyll's documents and it is suggested that Bayes rather enhanced his account.

Dick Turpin found posthumous fame through sensationalist broadsheets published at the time of his death. These, in turn, inspired ballads and plays. In the nineteenth century, Turpin became a real star when he featured in a novel called *Rookwood*.

GLOSSARY TERMS

Words in **bold** in the text relate to Glossary entries, see p. 219.

INTRODUCTION

If you were asked to conjure up an image of a highwayman you would probably imagine a handsome man in knee breeches, long leather boots, a three-cornered hat, cloak and mask: a kind of romanticised style from the mid to late seventeenth century; for most of us this would be a true knight of the road.

We'd say he was a gentleman, courteous and pleasantly requesting that we hand over our valuables as if he was doing us a great favour and we should be thankful for it. But would this be anywhere near the truth of what a highwayman, or highwaywoman, really was?

The question is easy to answer when we begin to look at the desperate, violent men and women who stopped and robbed people travelling on the road and committed other felonies too; very few bound themselves solely to the highway. Some were determined criminals who belonged to ruthlessly cruel gangs. They had no respect for life and would kill for the fun of it. Others were drawn to highway robbery because they were incapable of settling to any hard labour or work that would tie them down to one place.

There were gamblers and drinkers (who would be classed as addicts these days), who had to rob in order to get quick money for the gaming tables or to pay debts to even bigger criminals than themselves. As Henry Fielding says, gambling is 'a school in which most Highwaymen of Eminence have been bred'. In Fielding's time, a great many highwaymen, perhaps not so many highwaywomen, were compulsive gamblers.

A few men and women were lured into highway robbery when they were drunk or they thought that they'd try it just once – their stories tend to be very short.

There were highway robbers in medieval times, Elizabethan times and many during the English Civil War, but highway robbery in England died out almost completely in the nineteenth century with the advent of railways and an established police force.

Depending on what era they came from, the men and women who were called highway robbers wore the clothes of their day, fashionable or not. Women dressed as men and at least one man dressed as a woman. Some wore masks and others went barefaced. They were usually mounted on a horse, but not exclusively; there were people convicted of highway robbery who committed their crimes on foot, sometimes as fellow passengers of those they robbed.

There were highwaymen and women in other countries, too. In Australia, they were called bushrangers and they proliferated right up to the beginning of the twentieth century. The Australian landscape was vast and rugged and travel was still mostly by horse and coach. In Spain, Italy and South America, there were bandits. In the wild North American West, highwaymen were known as knights of the road.

Sometimes these robbers acted as folk heroes: robbing the rich and giving to the poor, righting wrongs and fighting injustice. Mostly they were thugs who stole from whoever was unlucky enough to get in their way. Victims were often killed or badly beaten and left with nothing, not even their clothes.

Since the execution of some of the most notorious highway robbers, their exploits have been turned into fiction in the form of ballads, novels, plays and films. In common with pirates, highwaymen and women have become legendary icons: daring, fearless justice seekers or plain, lovable rogues.

In an attempt to add truth to the fairy tales, this book documents the well-known, lesser-known and almost-unknown men and women who were, at some time in their lives, accused of highway robbery. I have taken, where possible, contemporary or near-contemporary accounts of these legendary figures, but sometimes it is not easy to get to the real person behind the mask.

TIMELINE

1066 Battle of Hastings
1196 First recorded execution on the site that would become Tyburn gallows
1284 Birth of Edward II
1312 Birth of Edward III
1327 Death of Edward II
1377 Death of Edward III
1405 Possible birth of Sir Thomas Malory of Newbold Revel, supposed author of *Le Morte d'Arthur* and notorious highwayman
1471 Death of Sir Thomas Malory of natural causes
1485 End of the War of the Roses with Henry Tudor becoming Henry VII
1491 Birth of Henry VIII
1509 Death of Henry VII; His son, Henry VIII, becomes king
1533 Birth of Elizabeth I
1534 Henry VIII breaks with the Roman Catholic Church
1536 The Pilgrimage of Grace rebellion starts in the north in protest against the religious reforms taking place
1537 Leading members of the Pilgrimage of Grace executed on the orders of Henry VIII
1547 Death of Henry VIII; His young son, Edward VI, becomes king
1553 Death of Edward VI; Mary, Catholic daughter of Henry VIII, gets the throne

1558 Elizabeth, Protestant daughter of Henry VIII, becomes Elizabeth I of England

1566 Birth of James I of England

1571 Tyburn 'Tree' scaffold erected in Tyburn

1588 Defeat of the Spanish Armada

1589 Birth of Moll Cutpurse (Mary Firth)

1599 Birth of Oliver Cromwell

1600 Birth of Charles I

1603 Death of Elizabeth I

1611 Birth of Sawney Douglas; Translation of the bible in English (the King James Bible)

1614 Birth of Isaac Atkinson

1618 Possible birth of Captain James Hind

1620 Possible birth of Captain Zachary Howard

1624 Birth of Gilder-Roy

1625 Death of James I; Charles I crowned King of England

1630 Birth of Charles II

1633 Birth of James II

1634 Birth of Katherine Ferrers

1640 Execution of Isaac Atkinson

1642 Outbreak of the English Civil War

1643 Birth of Claude Duval

1649 Beheading of Charles I

1650 Execution of Patrick Flemming

1651 End of the English Civil War

1652 Execution of Captain Zachary Howard; Execution of Captain James Hind

1653 Oliver Cromwell named Lord Protector

1654 Birth of Tom Rowland

1656 Birth of Joan Bracey

1658 Death of Oliver Cromwell; Execution of Gilder-Roy

1660 Death of Katherine Ferrers

1661 Charles II, King of England, has Cromwell's disinterred body hung from the gallows tree at Tyburn

1663 Death of Moll Cutpurse (Mary Frith)

1664 Execution of Sawney Douglas
1666 Great Fire of London
1670 Execution of Claude Duval
1675 Birth of James Leonard
1679 Birth of Robert Drummond
1681 Birth of John Smith
1683 Birth of Ned Wicks
1685 Executions of Edward and Joan Bracey
1685 Death of Charles II; James II crowned King
     of England
1686 Birth of Francis Bailey; Birth of John Everett
1687 Birth of James Wright
1688 Birth of Jack Addison; Birth of William Colthouse;
     Birth of William Burridge
1689 Execution of William Bew; Birth of James Drummond
1690 Birth of William Barton
1691 Birth of John Young
1692 Birth of Nathaniel Jackson
1693 Execution of James Leonard
1694 Birth of Humphrey Angier; Execution of Tom Austin
1695 Birth of James Carrick
1697 Birth of Thomas Polson
1698 Birth of Anthony Drury; Birth of William Duce; Birth
     of John Dykes; Birth of John Dyer
1699 Birth of James Harman; Birth of William Marple;
     Execution of Tom Rowland
1700 Birth of Mary Young (Jenny Diver); Birth of
     Ferdinando Shrimpton; Birth of Joseph Blake; Birth of
     William Burk
1701 Death of James II
1702 Birth of William Sperry
1704 Birth of Timothy Cotton; Execution of John Smith
1705 Richard Turpin baptised
1711 Execution of Jack Addison
1713 Execution of Ned Bonnet; Execution of Ned Wicks

1721 Execution of William Barton; Execution of John Dykes; Execution of James Wright

1722 Execution of William Burridge; Execution of James Carrick; Execution of William Colthouse; Execution of Nathaniel Jackson; Execution of John Molony

1723 Execution of William Duce; Execution of Humphrey Angier; Execution of William Burk

1724 Execution of Stephen Gardiner; Execution of Joseph Blake

1725 Execution of James Harman; Execution of Francis Bailey; Execution of William Sperry

1726 Possible death of Mary Blacket; Execution of Anthony Drury

1729 Executions of William Marple and Timothy Cotton; Execution of James Drummond; Execution of John Dyer; Execution of John Everett

1730 Execution of Ferdinando Shrimpton; Execution of Robert Drummond; Execution of John Doyle; Execution of Thomas Polson; Execution of John Young

1739 Execution of Richard 'Dick' Turpin; Richard Bayes writes *The Genuine History of the Life of Richard Turpin*

1741 Execution of Mary Young (Jenny Diver)

1765 Birth of Mary Bryant

1774 Execution of John Rann (Sixteen String Jack)

1778 Mary Bryant put on board the First Fleet to be transported to Australia

1783 Tyburn gallows sees its last public hanging with the execution of the highwayman John Austin

1791 Mary Bryant and family steal a boat and flee Australia

1793 Mary Bryant receives a pardon with the help of James Boswell

1800 Execution of Richard Ferguson

1803 Execution of Robert Smith

1807 John Forsyth patents his percussion system firearms

PART 1

A HISTORY OF HIGHWAYMEN AND HIGHWAYWOMEN

WHAT IS A
HIGHWAYMAN?

He'd a French cocked hat on his forehead, and a bunch of lace
    at his chin;
He'd a coat of the claret velvet, and breeches of fine doe-skin.
They fitted with never a wrinkle; his boots were up to his thigh!
And he rode with a jewelled twinkle
His rapier hilt a-twinkle
His pistol butts a-twinkle, under the jewelled sky.

When we speak of a highwayman, or highwaywoman, we conjure up a specific figure that looks like the man out of Alfred Noyes's famous poem. This, though, is only one type of highway robber, one that came from the mid to late eighteenth century. It is the clothes, in this instance, that maketh the highwayman or highwaywoman (the wicked lady of legend and film was also dressed in this style).

Robin Hood was a highwayman. He was not called such; but he was an outlaw, if not your average robber. He had an axe to grind with the wicked politicians of the day. That isn't to say that some of his victims wouldn't have been highly traumatised by the ordeal or that they all deserved what they got. Robin Hood, ultimately, fits into the highway robbery bracket because he performed a specific type of theft. The word 'rob' originally comes from a word of German origin, *raub*,

A highwayman came riding.

meaning 'theft'. It came into English from the Latin, *deraubare*.
To rob is, therefore, to thieve. Highway robbery is the theft of
one person's belongings by another with the intent of depriv-
ing the owner of them permanently.

The common law definition concerning robbery used to be:

> Robbery is the felonious and violent taking of money or goods
> from the person of another, putting him in fear, be the value
> thereof above or under one shilling.

Robin Hood.

Highway robbery was theft, with the intention of using fear on the victim, committed on the street, road or field; it didn't literally have to take place on a main road. We can include Robin Hood to the brother and sisterhood of highway robbery because that was where Robin committed his thefts: outside, in the open air of a public place.

The term 'highwayman' is thought to have come into common use in the early part of the seventeenth century. Men and women who have committed highway robbery have, for the most part, been very ordinary looking people: no romantic black coat, three-cornered hat or ruffles of lace. Very often, the robbery was not premeditated but an act of desperation made on a whim or because an opportunity arose. There were, however, organised highway robbers; some working in gangs, some in pairs and others always alone. Within the gangs, the main perpetrators of the actual robberies were men and the women would fence the goods to pawnbrokers or other outlets.

A few women did go out deliberately on the open road to point their pistols at coaches and demand the passengers to 'Stand and deliver!'. However, the stories of most women who were indicted for highway robbery were often quite banal: petty theft taken one step further.

Highway robbery had its heyday from the time of the English Civil War to the middle of the eighteenth century. After that, it began to wane. The last recorded highway robbery in England took place in 1831. The crime of mounted robbery continued much later in countries like Australia and America.

HIGHWAYMEN IN OTHER COUNTRIES

Robbery committed in the open air, usually targeting travellers, was a world-wide phenomenon. In Australia, there were bushrangers and, in general, they have received a similar, romantic gloss to the English highwaymen. Their crimes are seen as deeds, their escapes as daring adventures and their rugged lifestyles as manly and heroic.

Famous names abound in the world of bushrangers (who hasn't heard of Ned Kelly, the Australian equivalent of Dick Turpin and Claude Duval?) and Australians are well aware of

A bushranger in a cabbage-tree hat.

Ben Hall, Frank Gardiner and Captain Thunderbolt (whose hideout is a twenty-minute drive from my home town).

The Australian bushrangers worked in much the same manner as the highwaymen. They ambushed coaches and threatened to kill all the travellers, including the coachman and any guards, if valuables weren't handed over without resistance. They worked the highways of Australia from the beginnings of its colonisation in 1788 until the execution of Ned Kelly in 1880. One of the very first convicts sent to Australia on the First Fleet was a woman from England convicted of highway robbery. Her story is told later in this book.

The American West was another vast area that was in the process of being developed into towns and cities, and it faced similar problems to Australia. As people populated places across the continent, and supplies and travel could take days and weeks through wild lands, there were lots of opportunities for outlaws to waylay them and steal everything they had. In America these rascals were known as road agents. In South North America and Spain they were called bandits. France had *brigands*, Italy had *brigantes* and in Hungary they were *betyars*. In the Balkans and eastern Europe highwaymen were called *hajduk*.

In our own time, we still suffer highway robbery. In some countries little has changed in the way thieves ambush travellers, often tourists, and threaten them with guns and knives. In modern, first-world cities carjacking has become a common crime in which the vehicle itself is taken, often with the victim in the driver's seat driving to the directions of the thief.

THE LAW, PRISONS AND SENTENCES

In the early days of apprehending criminals there were no policemen. There were soldiers, guards and ordinary citizens who could grab hold of an offender and drag them to a place of confinement. To be accused of stealing goods worth more than 1s meant an arrest, a hearing, a trial and then, if found guilty by a jury, sentencing, which could result in hanging.

In Tudor times, a system of watchmen and constables was established. Members of the community volunteered or were selected to work on a roster with no pay to keep the streets of their villages and towns safe from criminals. Similarly, during the eighteenth century, a class of men (possibly including women) was established known as thief-takers. They were civilians who were hired by victims of crime to hunt down and capture those that they suspected had wronged them. This system, like any other, led to a great deal of corruption. Jonathon Wild, in the 1720s, was known as the Thief-Taker General and in this position he was able to continue and expand his own criminal empire. One of the scams he worked was to have his gang members steal goods and then return them to the owner to get the reward or fee. No one was safe from Wild. He would turn in his own employees to aid his disguise as an upstanding citizen. In 1725, Wild himself was taken, tried and hanged.

*Jonathon Wild in
Newgate prison.*

It wasn't until 1829 that the beginnings of a professional police force emerged at the instigation of Sir Robert Peel. They functioned largely as a preventative force and were known as the London Metropolitan Police.

PRISONS

Where were these accused felons taken after their arrest? In the time of Robin Hood, they would be put in the dungeon of the local castle or fortress. Later, they were put in prison. In London there were a number of prisons of different quality and security to suit different crimes. There were debtors' prisons, which were generally low security for housing men, women and complete families who were in debt. The debtor had to stay in prison, though the family was free to come and go, until they paid their debts and a prison fine as well. This was a bit difficult to do if you were locked up in gaol, so debts had to be paid by friends and relatives. It was this kind of prison – Marshalsea – that was the birthplace of Dickens's Little Dorrit, and it was where she remained until she was an adult.

Newgate prison.

Other prisons include **Poultry Compter** in Cheapside, named after the livestock sold in the area, and Bridewell Palace, originally one of Henry VIII's houses. In 1553, Edward VI gave the building to the City of London to be used as a poorhouse. In 1556, it also became a prison, hospital and workhouse. Bridewell did not house hardened criminals, but acted more as a place to home the impoverished. A good many debtors ended up in Bridewell. The name was used by similar prisons across England, Scotland and Ireland. The building was destroyed in the Great Fire of London only to be rebuilt in 1666–67. By 1863, it was completely pulled down.

And then there was Newgate. This prison was for true criminals who were a danger to the public and needed to be secured so that they couldn't escape. Many of Newgate's inmates left only to face the gallows.

The system in gaol was quite different to how it is in today's prisons. The prisoner was fed the bare minimum unless they had private funds to pay for a better quality and quantity of food. The gaolers were open to corruption and for a few coins would do all sorts of favours for the prisoners (except, of course, releasing them).

Inmates awaiting trial, sentencing or execution could entertain visitors if they wanted. Notorious criminals, often highwaymen, attracted large audiences to hear stories of their adventures. The guards charged admittance for the privilege of hearing the tales from the criminal's own lips and made a nice little sum on the side.

TRANSPORTATION

England had an overcrowding problem in prisons that lasted for decades. One solution was to sentence criminals to transportation. This meant sending them overseas to a British colony to work for seven years. Before the discovery of

Australia, transportation involved going to the plantations in Virginia in America. Several of the highway robbers featured in this book, both men and women, suffered this fate. Once Australia was on the map, convicts were sent there instead. One of those convicted of highway robbery, amongst other things, was Mary Bryant, who became one of the first prisoners to be sent to the brand-new colony.

Transportation was the soft option. Sometimes, perhaps if it was a first offence, convicted criminals would have their death sentences lessened to one of transportation for seven years. The idea was to give the person a second chance. If the colonies didn't kill them off they would be only too grateful to be able to leave those far-flung places and return home, punished enough never to offend again.

If a prisoner returned before their seven years were up and they were caught, the sentence was automatically one of death. It didn't always happen quite like that, though. There were petitions made on behalf of prisoners, juries could take pity on the accused, pardons could be granted and even escapes made.

EXECUTION

Execution was the ultimate punishment; there was no coming back from being hanged by the neck until you were dead (except for a couple of interesting cases). Death, however, didn't always follow the sentence; a prisoner could receive a pardon before the execution took place or they could escape.

The method of hanging at Tyburn, the short drop method, ensured that you choked to death. It could be a slow process and bodies were left to hang for several hours after execution to make sure that they were well and truly dead. The most notorious set of gallows in London, if not the whole of England, was at Tyburn.

The real effect of The
Newgate Calendar *on children.*

Before a criminal got as far as begin either transported
or hanged at Tyburn, they were taken to the Old Bailey, the
Central Criminal Court of England. Conveniently, the court
was housed next door to Newgate prison. The original building was destroyed in the Great Fire of London, but was rebuilt
some years afterwards as an open-air court in an attempt to
stop the spread of disease. In 1734 it was enclosed, but in
1750 sixty people died of Typhus, including the Lord Mayor
of London. The cause was the unsanitary condition of the
Old Bailey. The court was rebuilt yet again in 1750 and further developed in 1824.

Once arrested, the criminal would stand trial before the
judge and a jury. The jury would decide whether the accused
was innocent or guilty and the judge would determine the
sentence. If the guilty party was sentenced to death then they
would go back and wait in Newgate for the next hanging date
at Tyburn.

TYBURN

Tyburn was a name that struck terror into the hearts of all serious criminals for centuries. It was the last place that a condemned man would breathe air before a heavy rope, tied in its artful knot, was placed around their neck. Tyburn was a village that took its name from the stream bearing the same name, a tributary of the Thames. It was an important place for several reasons. It was from Tyburn Springs that Sir Gilbert de Sanford, who owned the village, agreed to let London pipe water for its citizens. The water ran along an intricate system of lead pipes that ran through the city to Cheapside and into a public conduit for free public consumption.

Tyburn witnessed its first public execution as early as 1196 when William Fitz Osbert was stripped naked, dragged behind a horse to Tyburn and hanged for his part in giving the poverty stricken people of the city a public voice. He was seen as a troublemaker and rebel: a threat to the throne and the comfort of every well-off person in London.

In the time of Henry VIII, Tyburn was used again for hanging the leaders of a possible rebellion. The death of Nicholas Tempest, the king's bowbearer, is an example of this. He was executed for being an instrumental part in the Pilgrimage of Grace. Thirty-four years later, Tyburn became an official place of execution by hanging. In 1571, the 'Tyburn Tree', as they called the triple gallows, was erected for the purpose of mass executions. It was set right in the middle of the road in an unmistakable attempt to put fear into all who might be tempted to turn to crime.

Elizabeth I had Dr John Story hanged from the Tree. He was a Catholic who would not acknowledge her as the true monarch of England; he was also the tree's first customer.

Later, when Charles II had ascended the throne, certain enemies of the Crown, Oliver Cromwell included, were

Tyburn gallows.

disinterred and hanged from the gallows as a symbol of the King of England's authority and sacredness: the men who beheaded Charles I were treated like common murderers.

As the executions became more frequent they attracted a growing crowd of spectators. Stands for the audience, also known as Mother Proctor's Pews, were erected for the comfort of the public (at a cost, of course) and refreshments were sold. The stands were easily overcrowded and one of them later collapsed, killing many of the people on it. It was nevertheless an early and extremely popular form of tourist attraction. In fact, on execution days (along with festive days), apprentices were allowed the time to go and witness them.

The days set for Tyburn executions had to correspond to the days that the local assizes were held. This meant that there could only be up to eight days a year on which hangings could be performed. When they did take place, it was a real spectacle with the trip from Newgate prison to the Tyburn Tree taking up to three hours, despite being only 2 miles away. Revellers would watch as the convoy (which could consist of several open carts and a mourning coach) would arrive accompanied by an armed guard. Criminals who had no money went in the open carts, dressed in simple linen shifts or clothes, perched on top of their own coffins for all to see, but some of the richer ones were able to go in the mourning coach dressed in black silk or satin. The convoy would make comfort stops along the route to let the condemned prisoners have refreshments before their last ordeal.

The last criminal to be hanged on Tyburn Tree was, fittingly, a highwayman called John Austin in 1783.

COSTUMES
AND WEAPONS

COSTUMES

The timeline for highway robbery spans centuries: too many to show the range of clothes that the robbers would have worn. Instead, we'll concentrate on those couple of hundred years in which the highway robber was most prevalent.

The seventeenth century saw the rise of the highwayman and highwaywoman as England's bloody Civil War dominated the middle decades. Two very different factions arose with two completely different sets of political and cultural beliefs. The old system, that of monarchy, was disposed of and the Parliamentarians took the place of the king. The leader of this group was Oliver Cromwell. His soldiers came to be known as Roundheads on account of the distinctive bowl-shaped helmets they wore.

Oliver Cromwell.

A Cavalier.

The Cavaliers, as the opposing Royalist soldiers were called, wore lavish outfits with lace trims and plumed hats to reflect the aristocratic state that they had enjoyed and hoped to enjoy again once the war had been won.

There were highwaymen and women from both camps. On the Royalist side, there were men and women who had had their estates seized by order of the new regime. They were on the run, living with friends or relatives who had been lucky enough to keep a low profile and, therefore, of roofs over their heads. Many of the men had rewards posted for their capture and so life was always on the move and there was no means of making a proper living.

Several of the best-known highwaymen came from this background. Not only did they rob to feed themselves, but they swore oaths to not let a regicide live. They targeted the Parliamentarians.

On the other side, we see soldiers fighting for Parliament finding themselves at a loose end when fighting ceased. There were no rewards for the common man and when the monarchy was reinstated their past was not in their favour. Many of these soldiers had come from working-class families who had supported the deposition of Charles I because of the lack of help he had offered them in their struggle for basic necessities; they would have nothing to fall back on when these hard times returned. Those soldiers who had signed up young would not have had a chance to learn a trade, others would have been bitter that they were abandoned again.

So, in looking at a typical highwayperson's outfit there is a problem; one size does not fit all. Republican soldiers would have been very plainly dressed, even in rags sometimes. Clothes would also be stolen from travellers or from breaking into houses. Clothing would also be deliberately used for disguise, as in the case of at least one highwayman who dressed as a woman when committing robberies to throw the law off his scent.

Women committing highway robbery probably wore their everyday working clothes. Many of these women, unless they were of aristocratic birth and robbing for the king, were just poor people trying to earn a little extra.

Katherine Ferrers, the Wicked Lady, gave to the female highway robber the glamour that Claude Duval, Dick Turpin and the like gave to the male highway robber. She is supposed to have kept a suit of men's clothes specifically for the purpose of robbing. It was hidden in a secret room, if the tales are true, and consisted of a tricorn hat and a long black coat, over which was worn a cloak. She donned a half-mask and wore a large scarf wound around the bottom half of her face. She abandoned skirts for more practical breeches.

During the time of the Civil War, both men and women on the king's side wore their hair long, or covered short hair with a luxurious wig, although the general wearing of these didn't fully come in until 1660 and the return of Charles II. The long, natural-looking locks would fall below the shoulders and one lock would be brought forward and tied with a bow at the end.

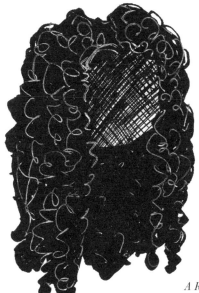

A Restoration-style wig.

Women's hairstyle during the English Civil War.

The portrait of 14-year-old Katherine Ferrers shows a distinctive style for women in which the hair from the forehead is pulled back over a roll and ringlets hang down either side to frame the face. A very short fringe might have been left and curled tightly over the forehead.

Men on the side of Parliament wore their hair cropped short in the Puritan mode or longish, but without the romantic lock of hair falling over the shoulder with its little bow. Many working-class men wore a simple shoulder-length bob.

Hats were worn by people of all classes and political persuasions. The tricorn, or three-cornered hat, supposedly part of the Wicked Lady's costume, would actually have been an anachronism in her day. This elegant hat didn't appear until well after the return of Charles II, probably not until 1690.

Three-cornered hat.

Soft, felt hat.

A similar option was a soft, felt hat with a long, wide brim that was often decorated with feathers. It was the hat of the Cavalier and it was much more likely the type of hat that Katherine Ferrers would have worn.

Roundhead soldiers were so called because of the shape of the metal helmets they wore. These were helmets without frivolity, which had a round dome, a peak at the front and a neck and side flaps. A Roundhead would have worn woollen knee breeches and a woollen doublet adorned with a plain, white linen collar and sturdy, long leather boots, minus the elaborate bucket top of the Cavaliers.

Over the doublet, the Roundhead soldier would have worn a sleeveless, leather jerkin, which is a bit like a long waistcoat. It may have had little caps over the armholes. Over all this, he wore a metal breastplate with a simple metal skirt attached. He may have also had long, woollen hose pulled up to his breeches.

37

Roundhead soldier in uniform.

Clothes for women throughout the seventeenth century tended to be heavy and cumbersome. They had lost the farthingale of Queen Elizabeth I's time and, in general, the dress was simpler. About the time of the Civil War, skirts had a natural waistline. Later, with the return of the monarchy to the throne, a deep V-shape appeared at the front of the skirt (often decorated with small tabs all around it or some other trim) in an updated version of the old queen's stomacher-style gowns.

Women's dress during the English Civil War.

Mid-century skirts could be closed or open at the front to reveal a patterned underskirt. Overskirts were often looped up in a number of ways to produce a ruffled effect. Necklines were low, wide and square. The otherwise bare flesh was often covered

Cavalier and puritan collars.

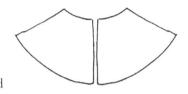

with a kerchief of fine cotton or linen. Collars, when used, were large and either plain white for the Puritans or made entirely of lace or trimmed with lace for the Royalists.

Working class and peasant women wore what was available. Often clothes were handed down through the generations, altered by each recipient as best they could to follow the basic fashion. A mid-century maid-servant would have worn a white cotton or linen shift over which she would have had a more sturdy bodice and gown. The bodice may well have been boned to make a fitted shape. It may have laced up the front in a decorative manner or up the back more discreetly. Over her head she would have a plain linen cap to keep her neat for work.

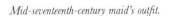

Mid-seventeenth-century maid's outfit.

When Charles II returned from exile and was restored to the English throne, fashions didn't dramatically alter. They did, however, take on a more decorative and frilly look. There was an abundance of lace, silk, satin and velvet: luxury fabrics for a luxury class of people.

Wigs became very popular, especially long, dark, curled wigs as were favoured by the king.

In the eighteenth century, fashions subtly changed again. For instance, women's skirts got wider and were held out with hoops. Men wore the tricorn hat for fifty years or more and wigs got shorter, more stylised and heavily powdered so that everyone looked prematurely grey.

Mid-eighteenth-century-style men's outfit.

Long, heavy boots were out for men unless they were travelling and then they tended to be a neater and closer fit. There was also, in general, a more tailored and refined air about clothes; colours tended to be paler and materials lighter.

At this time there was also a return to a pastoral idyll; the milk maid look was in. A soft, draped shift with rolled sleeves was worn under a fitted over-dress with a full skirt in a delicate floral or striped pattern. The waist was accentuated by a tightly laced bodice that also helped push up the bosom, and a linen apron was worn over the front of the skirt. It was a style worn by ordinary people, the working people, and copied by

Mid-eighteenth-century-style women's outfit.

the rich but in luxury fabrics with decorations. Hair was worn shorter or in neat, tighter buns. Mop caps came in, as well as headscarves worn under broad-brimmed straw or felt hats.

By the end of the eighteenth century, styles had become extravagant to the point of ridiculous. A woman's hair, or rather wig, was piled high and powdered. The dresses were broad skirts worn over panniers tied around the waist. Overskirts were often pulled up to the sides to reveal a gathered underskirt. There was also a style in which the overdress hung loose at the back from the shoulders; it was called a sack-back. Stripes and small flowers were in, as were dainty little shoes.

Men also wore powdered wigs, but they were shorter, tightly curled and had a little ponytail or plait at the back tied with a large bow. This is the style that modern barristers' and judges' wigs came from. Coats were tighter fitting and hose were smooth and fitted under similarly tight-fitting breeches.

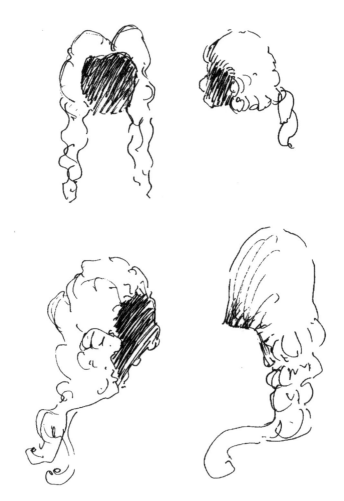

A selection of late eighteenth-century wigs for men and women.

From all these styles, highwaymen and highwaywomen could choose what they liked to wear during their working hours. It must be said, though, that it is unlikely that many of them chose the more outrageous or notable styles. Ease of wear and practicality would have had a large bearing on what they wore. Breeches and boots, for instance, would facilitate running or riding away. A large coat would have provided warmth on cold nights as well as a modicum of protection when fighting. They also were good for hiding pistols and their large pockets were essential for stowing the stolen goods. Hats were head protection as well as an aid in disguise. Probably, they were such a normal part of everyday wear that little was thought about them one way or another; one wore a hat when one went outside. Not to wear a hat would probably attract notice.

More important than the clothes they wore would have been the choice of weapon a highway robber used to threaten his or her victims, whether it was intended to be used or not.

WEAPONS

'Stand and deliver!' was the traditional call of the highwayman or highwaywoman when they stopped a traveller and attempted to rob him or her. What use are words, however, if there is no power to enforce them? A deadly weapon was needed to show that the robber meant business.

Usually, a pistol was produced, but sometimes it would be a rapier or, in one instance, a bill hook. But, what kind of pistols did the highway robber use and what are a rapier and a bill hook?

Pistols are handheld guns, as opposed to long-barrelled rifles that require the support of two arms. Highway robbers would have used **flintlock** pistols. The **flintlock** was a mechanism used for igniting and firing the gunpowder that

'Stand and deliver!'

would propel a metal ball from the gun's barrel. Before the seventeenth century, there were several other types of ignition: doglock, matchlock and wheellock.

The **flintlock** pistol was invented in the early part of the seventeenth century by a French watch- and lock-making family by the name of Bourgeoys. The **flintlock** worked by having a piece of flint held in place by a cock (the part of the gun that sits on top and is drawn backwards in order for it to be fired). When the trigger is pulled, the cock strikes down onto a piece of steel sitting above a pan holding gunpowder. The ensuing spark from flint on steel ignites the gunpowder, which is packed behind the bullet. These guns couldn't be reloaded quickly and were used in warfare for an initial charge before hand-to-hand combat, using swords of different kinds.

A flintlock mechanism.

The highwayman would have obtained his weapon in several ways. Many robbers were ex-soldiers and would have retained any weapons with which they had been issued when their commission ended or they deserted. Pistols were often stolen and they could also be bought on the second-hand market.

The **flintlock** was such a successful invention that it was used for well over 200 years in pistols and other small arms weaponry. However, while it was probably the most common weapon used in highway robbery, it had its disadvantages. One of these was the very short range. It was also notoriously inaccurate. Neither of these issues, however, would worry a highwayman or woman as he or she worked with the fear that the **flintlock** pistol could create in the victim just by pointing the weapon in their direction.

Another of the **flintlock's** improvements was to take the exterior cock and frizzen and put them into the interior of the pistol to reduce the problem of it catching on garments when the gun was pulled out of clothing. The guns were also smaller and could easily be hidden in the bearer's garments. In addition, pistols were produced to a very decorative design, particularly for ladies to carry for personal protection. There was a men's design that was much plainer as well.

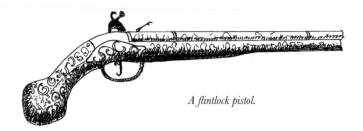

A flintlock pistol.

The **flintlock** was eventually replaced by the percussion system at the end of the eighteenth century and using gunpowder as the explosive was replaced by fulminate of mercury. This enabled the gun to be fired more rapidly. The inventor of this mechanism was a Scot by the name of Alexander John Forsyth (1768–1843) and he took out a patent for it in 1807. One of the advantages of the new system was that it could replace the **flintlock** workings of old pistols so that the purchase of a totally new weapon was unnecessary.

Another possibility for the highway robber was the revolver. The revolver would have been ignited by match, wheel or **flintlock**. The difference between the revolver and the standard pistol was that the revolver had a rotating barrel that carried a metal ball in each chamber. This meant that a number of shots could be fired in relatively quick succession. The primer in the pan still had to be renewed for each shot until the mid-seventeenth century when an Italian gunsmith invented an arrangement that used separate magazines for the powder and ball, which meant that it really could deliver a round of shots in a short amount of time. This invention was still in use in England up until the beginning of the nineteenth century.

While the weapon of choice for a highway robber would have been the easily concealed hand gun, such as a pistol or revolver, there would have been some who resorted to a rifle. The name rifle comes from the spiral groove made in the long

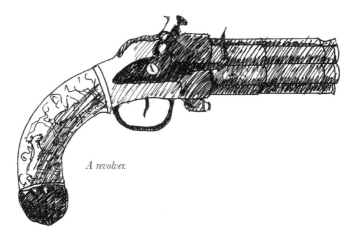

A revolver.

barrel of the gun. It meant that the ball was given a distinctive spin to it as it made its way up the barrel. This gave it a higher accuracy for finding its target, something that pistols did not have.

The **musket** evolved as a military weapon and it required powder to be carried with it at all times for reloading after each shot. The British army used a version of the **musket** called the Brown Bess. The gun had to have powder poured into the pan and some into the muzzle (the opening of the barrel out of which the bullet comes when fired) along with cartridge paper, it was then rammed down as far as it could go with a special rod. The musket ball went in afterwards and the gun had to be reloaded after each shot. A professional could shoot two or three times a minute.

As we shall read in some of the adventures of the highwaymen and highwaywomen, the **blunderbuss** was often carried as a weapon by men travelling on coaches. It's not always clear whether they thought that they'd defend themselves and their female companions with these weapons or whether they carried them for another purpose; either way, when it came to using them they were almost always

The musket with bayonet.

overpowered by the robbers. The **blunderbuss** was a short-range weapon with a distinctive bell-shaped muzzle, it generally had a **flintlock** mechanism.

Highwaymen not only used firearms but swords and daggers as well. Many of these would have seen active military service before they were used for holding up coaches. In battle, the sword was drawn after the **flintlock** had given up its one good shot. The sword carried by a highwayman or woman could have been a rapier or a cutlass. The first was a long, fine piece of steel with a sharp, pointy end for stabbing. The advantage of this was that the opponent was kept at arm's length. A cutlass had a shorter, curved blade, which was sharp along the outward curve and was used in a slashing motion to cut rather than pierce.

Daggers came in all shapes and sizes and could be used for everything from peeling an apple to threatening to slit a throat or stabbing someone through the heart. The dagger was easily concealed among clothing and didn't trip the wearer up as a long sword could (if the bearer wasn't properly trained in the art of using it).

Of course, this kind of weaponry wasn't available to all those who embarked on a highway career and there is one case of a robber using a bill hook. This is not a weapon at all but a short, sturdy hook that was used for laying hedges (cutting and interweaving the growing plants to form a dense barricade to keep livestock in and marauders out). There would have been other make-do weapons as well. Fists were often used, and boots to punch and kick a victim. Bayonets,

A rapier and a cutlass.

either mounted on the ends of rifles or removed and used as daggers, were not uncommon. There were reports of kitchen or butchers' knives; in fact, any weighty object that could be wielded as a weapon (a plank of wood or a rock, for instance) was an option. These were often used by the more ruthless or desperate criminals.

PART 2

LIVES OF HIGHWAYMEN
AND HIGHWAYWOMEN

JACK ADDISON

Born 1688 • Died 1711

Jack Addison was born near Lambeth. Nothing is known of his early childhood. As a youth he must have been apprenticed to a butcher, as this was recorded as his legitimate trade later in life. He also served as a soldier.

Like many criminals of the time, Addison took to theft as a means of supplementing an income that was inadequate to pay for his mistress and other luxuries. His first felonies were foot robberies and he worked with a gang. When he turned his attention to the highways, Addison displayed an admirable talent for quick and witty repartee. For example, when he engaged with a clergyman on the road between Westbourne Green and Paddington (after divesting the man of 5 guineas), he told the unhappy victim that the money was as safe in his pocket as in that of the original owner. The clergyman agreed and dared to ask for a small portion of the sum back to help him on his way. Addison responded with a grammatical riddle for the man to answer: 'If you can tell me what part of speech your gold is, I'll return it again.'

The clergyman said it was a noun substantive and explained why. Addison declared that he was wrong: 'I perceive you are no good grammarian, for where your gold is at present is a noun adjective, because it can be neither seen, felt, heard nor understood.' This seems to indicate that, somewhere along the line, Addison had received a thorough education in the basics of grammar.

Another victim of Addison's was the former landlord of the King's Head alehouse in King's Head. Again, the robbed man asked for a small part of it back so that he could get home. His request was denied.

'Had you been an honest tradesman,' Addison told him, 'perhaps I might have considered you, but as you know you wear a blue flag … because all of your profession neither eat, drink nor think but at other men's charges.'

To a lawyer he held up near Hampstead, on being warned that the lawyer would make sure Addison would get his just desserts when he eventually came to trial, the highwayman declared, 'I value not the severity of lawyers in England, who only learn to frame their cases by public riddles and imitating Merlin's prophecies, and so set all the Cross Row together by the ears; yet your whole law is not able to decide Lucian's old controversy betwixt *Tau* and *Sigma*.' The lawyer was then tied up and left beside the road.

On the whole, Addison displayed the romantic notion of the educated and gentlemanly rogue, using no physical violence, only threatening to blow a head off. He was glib with words and appeared to have read widely. He even displayed a sense of civic duty on the holding up of a sergeant of the **Poultry Compter**. Addison robbed him of 40*s* and not only refused to give the man any back again, but loudly upbraided him for being 'the spawn of a broken shop keeper, who takes delight in the ruin of thy fellow creatures! … the gallows is your purlieu, in which you and the hangman are quarter rangers; the one turns off, and the other cuts down.'

The sergeant's reply was that he hoped he'd have the pleasure of cutting Addison down. Before tying the sergeant up and leaving him on the roadside, Addison agreed that it might well come to that but not before the sergeant 'devoured a great many of the sheriff's custards first'.

Jack Addison had lived the life of the model highwayman, although his hold-ups on the road were always conducted on foot. He is reported to have made fifty-six robberies in this manner. However, in 1710, a former acquaintance and criminal, Will Jewel, gave information implicating Addison in a hold-up of the Duke d'Aumont, the French ambassador. Addison was arrested, taken to Newgate, tried and found guilty of a number of robberies committed on the king's highway. Addison was hanged at Tyburn on 2 March 1711 at the ripe old age of 23.

HUMPHREY ANGIER

Born *c.* 1694 • Died 1723

Humphrey Angier was born in Ireland in a village not far from Dublin. When he was old enough, he was apprenticed to a cooper in Cork. It was not a trade to the boy's liking and Angier refused to behave himself while employed by his master. He had also fallen in with a bad crowd, which exacerbated the relationship between himself and his employer. Instead of waiting to be given his marching orders, Angier left his position of his own accord. For up to four years afterwards, the cooper hired bodyguards to protect himself because he was afraid of being attacked by some of his former apprentice's mates. They were known to be criminals and he felt himself to be a target for robbery.

When Angier was 18, his father finally removed him from Cork and took him to England where his misdeeds would not taint the family's good name. At first, it looked as though the boy might settle down and clear his name, even make the family proud when he enlisted to fight for the king in Scotland during the Jacobite Uprising of 1715. It was, however, too much to hope for and he left not long after, returning to England to fall into his old habits. It was back in London that he became acquainted with the notorious highway robber William Duce, whose misdeeds are also documented in this book. Angier eventually married Duce's sister, bringing the two criminals together like brothers, and together with the rest of the gang they embarked on a series of violent robberies.

There was nothing at all gentlemanly about Angier. Some of his companions, however, were far worse, not only robbing with physical violence but also murdering victims for the fun of it. Angier once recounted a story, purportedly told to him by two of Duce's gang members, Mead and Butler, of how they had met a newly married cobbler on the road who was on his way to visit friends. Mead and Butler had lured him off the road where they then bound, gagged and robbed him. Pretending that this was all that they were going to do to him, the two rode off, but they had no intention of leaving the poor man alone; they doubled back and shot him through the head. Angier claimed he was sickened by the delight that these men took in their cruelty and refused to treat them as companions after he heard their tale, although he wasn't brave enough to hand them over to the authorities for murder.

Whether this episode and similar ones turned Angier away from the life of a criminal or whether his wife wanted a settled life is not known, but soon after the couple set up an alehouse at Charing Cross. Unfortunately, but not surprisingly, the business soon attracted rough customers and gained a reputation as a thieves' den.

It would be nice to think that Angier and his wife had intended to ply an honest trade with their establishment, but it was not to be so. There were temptations too attractive for either of them to resist. In one instance, the pair colluded to rob a drunken Irishwoman. Angier carried the prone woman upstairs and pretended that he wanted to make love to her. They were interrupted by Angier's 'outraged' wife, who pulled the woman off her bed and picked her pocket while she did so.

It is not difficult to understand why, within a remarkably short time, Angier was compelled to close up shop and move elsewhere as he and his disreputable patrons were drawing the attention of the law.

The couple's next business venture was a brandy shop, but they found that they had the same trouble, with their former clientele following them. It was in this shop that the law caught up with Angier. The business involving the Irishwoman and a crime in which Angier was not involved (a theft committed by a Dutch woman in the bar) were blamed on him and one of the maids working for him. They were tried at the Old Bailey, but the evidence was too weak to get a conviction. Both were released.

After this, Angier lost his business, decided to go back to highway robbery and took up with a new bunch of thieves: Carrick, Carrol, Lock and Kelly (more on these later). Some of these men stooped to the lowly activity of pickpocketing, which Angier at least pretended he was above. Later, however, when Angier was in gaol, he was beset by people asking about their belongings, such as watches and **snuff boxes**. Apparently, one of Angier's gang had been a dextrous pickpocket but, as Angier told them, Kelly, the true culprit, had gone to America and was never coming back.

Angier had evaded the hangman's noose for years, even though he had been caught and held under suspicion of criminal acts. In each of these cases the authorities were not able to pin any of the crimes on the man and he was always released. When his bad deeds finally caught up with him, it was because Angier had been arrested for a crime of which he was actually innocent. A coachman had been robbed of his watch, among other things, and a young woman who held a grudge against Angier was caught in the act of trying to pawn it. When she was arrested she insisted that she wasn't the perpetrator of the robbery and that the real thief was Angier. He was taken into custody, only for the case against him to break down. This time, however, he was retained and tried for numerous other offences, and for these he was ultimately found guilty and sentenced to hang.

Angier expressed his repentance for his crimes sincerely and implored God to help him in his hour of need. When he ascended the scaffold he made a moving speech impeaching the onlookers to learn from his crimes and not be led into temptation as he had been. He also swore that while he had undoubtedly been a thief, he had never murdered anyone in the course of his robberies.

It is said that he put the noose over his head himself before his execution, which took place on the 9 September 1723 when he was 29 years old.

ISAAC ATKINSON

Born *c*. 1614 • Died 1640

Isaac Atkinson was born a gentleman's son and was given all the luxuries and opportunities that this offered. His family estate was at Farringdon in Berkshire and he received the kind of education that his social standing demanded, which included being enrolled at Brazen Nose College in Oxford. Unfortunately, Isaac followed the path of many of his peers and spent more time enjoying a hectic social life than studying. During his second year at university his father withdrew him and took him home to teach him how to manage the estate. This did not go down well with young Isaac, who refused to do his duties as the only son and heir to a large estate. As a result, Isaac's father threatened to disinherit him entirely, but instead told him to leave the house, go forth into the world and attempt to make something of himself. This ploy did not work in the way that his father had planned.

Isaac left his father's house with a small amount of money and made straight for London where he drank and gambled it away very quickly. When the money was gone he left the city and began his career in crime. It started with relatively small burglaries, just to help him get home again. Of course, he was not expecting any kind of warm welcome there, so, rather than raise his father's wrath, he broke into his ancestral home via the kitchen window when everyone had gone to bed.

Whether the boy was lucky or the family careless with their cash is unclear, but Isaac was able to help himself to £50 in silver and 120 **broad pieces** of gold. It is said that he then wrapped 5 **broad pieces** in paper on which he had penned the following verse:

> Sir, your son did often bully,
> Because he never read in Tully;

What parents teach they ought to practise,
And I confess your test exact is
'Tis just to turn it on yourself
Your Bible stands upon the shelf;
The gold is yours, if you unclose it;
Else I shall find the dear deposit
Safe in a place by all forgotten,
When you, good man, are dead and rotten.

Having placed the note in the Bible, Isaac took the best horse from his father's stable and set off back to London. Isaac's father was not amused and consequently turned the whole estate over to a more distant relative. The old man died not long afterwards.

To compound this young villain's crimes, it is reported that he stopped at the church at Uxbridge and heard the local vicar preach, 'For ye know that the day of the Lord cometh as a thief in the night'. Atkinson decided to make the preacher swallow his words and accosted him on his way home after the service, robbing him and telling him that such a maxim was not always true as there were plenty of thieves about in the daytime too. The poor victim was left tied up away from the path while Atkinson rode away with a silver watch and £1 18*s*.

When Atkinson met the Attorney General to Charles I (named Noy) upon the road, he recognised him and used a parody of legal jargon to demand the man's money. Noy complied with the request in a jovial manner, which probably had more to do with him not wanting to antagonise his assailant than because he actually found it funny. This was the beginning of a habit for which Atkinson earned a reputation: robbing lawyers.

His name spread as the scourge of the highway and he was reported to have taken over £3,000 from around 160 lawyers in a space of eight months. Who said crime doesn't pay?

Isaac Atkinson finally met his match in a woman sitting by the roadside, resting with her mare at Turnham Green. As he rode past her, he saw that she was holding a bag full of halfpennies. It was too tempting and he stopped, demanding that she hand it over. Instead, the woman threw the bag over the hedge and ran off in the direction of the town where she sought out the authorities and told them of her ordeal. Atkinson, more interested in the money than quietening the woman, jumped over the hedge himself in search of the booty. While he was recovering it his own horse ran off after the woman's mare.

Floundering in the field in footwear suited for riding not walking over rough ground, Atkinson could not escape in time and he was soon surrounded by men from the town. As he was held at bay he took out his pistols and, in his desperation to escape, shot and killed four of the men. Despite his armed state, he was captured by the remaining mob and carried off to Newgate prison.

Isaac Atkinson showed no remorse for his bad behaviour and criminal activities and remained ill-mannered to all around him, which won him no favours within the gaol. Insolence, however, may have been a way to cover the terror that engulfed him because he tried to commit suicide by stabbing himself on the day of his execution. As the attempt was a dismal failure and did little more than inflict a flesh wound, he was simply bandaged and sent forth to the gallows.

Before they tied the noose, Atkinson is supposed to have said, 'Gentlemen, there's nothing like a merry life, and a short one.'

TOM AUSTIN

Birthdate Unknown • Died 1694

The crimes committed by this highwayman give the brotherhood a very bad name. There was nothing heroic, gentlemanly or brave in his sordid deeds.

Austin had a prosperous start in life. His family left him the sole heir of their farm plus an income of £80 a year. With such a good foundation before him and excellent prospects ahead of him, Austin soon found a wife who had a suitable fortune of £800. This was ready money for which he did not need to work. He spent it immediately and recklessly, so that four years after his marriage he was obliged to mortgage the estate.

His criminal activities began with fraud perpetrated against friends and neighbours who were good enough to forgive him, at least for his wife's sake if not his own. But the money he got through deception was not enough to cover his debts or his appetite for loose living and he soon set out as a highwayman.

The number of attacks performed by Austin isn't recorded, but on one occasion, and it may have been his only one, he held up the coach of Sir Zachary Wilmot on the road between Wellington and Taunton Dean. During the ensuing struggle, Wilmot was killed and Austin got away with 46 guineas and a silver-hilted sword. He was not discovered as the murderer and spent the money without any worry.

When funds were short, Austin went to visit his uncle who lived a mile from his own house. Only his aunt and young cousins were at home and they invited him to stay with them while they waited for his uncle to come home. After waiting a short while, Austin suddenly jumped up, seized a hatchet and butchered the family. He piled the bodies in one bloody heap and went upstairs to help himself to whatever money was available, which was only £60.

On his return to his own home, his wife questioned him about the blood on his shirt. It is stated that he called her a bitch and slit her throat then disembowelled his own two young children, bringing the massacre to nine people, seven of them children.

Austin was caught by his uncle who was dropping in on his own way home. When he saw the bloody knife in his nephew's hand and the dead bodies around him, he seized and bound him before calling for help to take him to gaol. At that stage the poor man did not know what was waiting for him in his own house.

Austin was hanged in August 1694.

FRANCIS BAILEY

Born *c.* 1686 • Died 1725

Francis Bailey was born in Worcestershire into extreme poverty and, consequently, he received little or no formal education. When he was old enough, his parents had him apprenticed to a local baker. It seemed as though the boy was going to make a good and honest living at baking bread; his master obviously thought so and put a lot of time and effort into his training. Nevertheless, as soon as he was able, Francis Bailey quit his position to become a soldier.

The life of a soldier suited Bailey very well and through his diligence he rose to the station of corporal and then to that of sergeant. He remained in the army for about twenty years, what would normally be the good part of a man's working life. To all outward appearances, Francis Bailey was an honest and law-abiding citizen.

However, this was no more than an act with which to cover his true vocation, that of highway robbery. How long Bailey had been engaged in this second job is not known, although he claimed that the idea first came to him on hearing a fellow soldier's tales of a highwayman with whom he had been friends. The stories were full of daring exploits, excitement and money enough to enable the robber to set himself up in business in Jamaica. It was a tale that stirred Bailey into action to try something similar.

Bailey's first victim was a vicar travelling alone by horse. The attempt soon backfired and the clergyman turned on Bailey, knocking him off his horse and riding away post-haste, leaving Bailey somewhat disconcerted but undeterred. He remounted his horse as soon as he could and set off after another target.

His first successful robbery occurred when he met with a wagon carrying four young women, accompanied by several young men, on their way to visit relatives in the country. These people put up no resistance and were robbed of £7 or so.

For most of his criminal life, Bailey worked exclusively alone. After his incident with the clergyman he was also always very quick to get away from the scene of his robberies.

Toward the end of his life, Bailey was on the brink of forming a partnership with another highwayman. However, on the day that they were to seal their business, the other party, an Irishman, was shot and badly wounded in an attempt to rob a coach on his own. When Bailey finally caught up with him the man was dying.

Not long after Bailey was arrested on charges of housebreaking and burglary, for which he insisted he was perfectly innocent. Perhaps the nearness of death and the idea of eternal suffering did something to Bailey's conscience, for while in gaol he confessed to numerous other crimes and worse ones. Despite the fact he remained adamant that he had never in his life broken into someone's home, it was for this offence that he was found guilty and sentenced to death.

Francis Bailey was hanged at Tyburn on 14 March 1725.

WILLIAM BARTON

Born *c.* 1690 • Died 1721

The story for many highwaymen is that they were born into families, rich or poor, of law-abiding and church-going citizens who tried hard to give their sons and daughters a decent start in life. In contrast, in William Barton we have a case where the son seems to have followed in the footsteps of his no-good father.

What Barton's father really did with himself is largely conjecture, as he left William's mother when William was a young boy and left for Jamaica to build a new life there, intending to set up a plantation. This wouldn't have been considered so wrong in itself, except that he took along a female companion who was not his wife.

William's mother took herself and her child to her parents' home where the boy's grandfather loved him and spoilt him as a grandfather should. The grandfather owned a large, reputable and popular eating house at Covent Garden. William was a favourite with the clientele and, though his father was absent, William had a stable and loving father figure in his grandfather. In fact, he had all the things that supposedly help a child become a well-balanced and responsible adult.

Despite these advantages William didn't settle down to work with his grandfather in the family business; he developed wanderlust, just as his father had done, and eventually went to Jamaica in search of him.

William arrived in the West Indies to find that his father had died and had not left him an enormous fortune at all. He then returned to sea to seek his fortune there instead. But instead of fortune he found adventure; the ship he was on was seized by the Spanish and its crew, cargo and passengers were sent to Spain as prisoners.

A Spanish prison is no better than an English one, and possibly worse, especially when the inmates may be innocent of criminal activity, as William Barton was. The food was sparse and of poor quality, the gaolers were not friendly and the conditions were harsh. William constantly planned his escape.

Fortune eventually favoured him when he and some of his fellow inmates were sent to mend an outer wall of the prison. This was the opportunity that they had been waiting for and, while under the pretence of building up the foundations, William and another prisoner, having stolen a guard's pouch, made a bomb out of the gunpowder, which they placed under the newly built section of wall. When they ignited it, it blew up a good couple of yards of the wall and Barton and some of the other prisoners ran through it during the ensuing uproar.

The escapees fled straight to a monastery where they were given refuge. The monastery offered a safe haven where they were hidden from the guards who were searching for them; it provided good food, clothing and shelter. In return, the prisoners worked in the monastery. Yet this refuge, although more comfortable, soon became another prison. One night, Barton and another Englishman managed to break out and reach an English ship fortuitously moored in the harbour below them.

Later, they discovered from the captain of the ship that he had been engaged by the monks to remove the English refugees from Spain anyway.

Back in England, Barton enlisted in the army and was shortly sent to Flanders to fight there. He gained a reputation as being a brave and reliable soldier and it looked as though his career was set; he had at last found employment that suited his adventurous spirit. It did not last. The war ended just as he was about to be made a paymaster-sergeant and he, along with many of his compatriots, were back in their native land looking for a way to earn a living. And by this time he had also acquired a rather high maintenance wife.

William's answer to unemployment was to become a highwayman. For one of his first campaigns (having heard the story of the pirate and Alexander the Great, with its conclusion being that the only difference between them was the size of the booty) William Barton sent along one of his men to check out the passengers in an oncoming coach. The word came back that it carried four young men armed with **blunderbusses** accompanying two young ladies, all of whom were served by a single footman.

The prospect of four loaded **blunderbusses** was no deterrent and Will hastily formed a plan of action. His partner was to ride up behind the coach and shoot a pistol over it to bring it to a halt. When this was done, Barton rode up to the front of it and demanded that the occupants 'Stand and deliver!'. The four gentlemen didn't raise a single firearm, but gave up over £100 between them. Barton then bade them to give him their guns as they obviously had no use for them.

Barton continued to live in this style until one day he attempted a robbery in Covent Garden. It was a bold but foolish move, as he was well known in that area and easy to trace. Once arrested, he was taken to Newgate prison to await trial.

William Barton was a lucky man. He'd been caught for attempted robbery, but he didn't get a death sentence to hang by the neck. Instead, he was to be transported for a period of seven years to His Majesty's New World colonies to work on the plantations there. Ever one to make the most of his situation, Barton, having been bought by a planter, soon became an indispensable servant. He worked as a plantation manager, overseeing the slaves and taking care of the farm when his master was away.

Barton could have made himself a comfortable life in the New World but he missed his wife and his homeland to such an extent that he decided to return there before his sentence was fulfilled. It didn't take much of an effort for him to run away from his master and find passage on a ship bound for

England. When he finally arrived in England, the first thing he did was seek out his wife and set up home again. And, once again, he took to the highway to make a living for both of them. All through his latter trials, Barton insisted that his wife had never played any part in the robberies or fencing of the stolen goods, or indeed that she had any knowledge whatsoever of how he earned their keep.

William's last robbery was made upon a coach carrying the Lord Viscount Lisbourne of Ireland and a lady passenger. He took a silver-hilted sword, a **snuff box** and 12*s*. He was caught, tried and sentenced to death. Not only had he been convicted of highway robbery, but he had broken the terms of his first sentence, to spend seven years in the colonies. Barton was resigned to the fact that he would die and set about putting his affairs in order. He made sure that relatives would take in his beloved wife and their daughter, leaving them wanting for nothing. He then began to prepare his soul for its next life.

Barton took to reading books to help his repentance in the eyes of God and was hanged on Friday 12 May 1721.

TIMOTHY BENSON

Birthdate Unknown • Date of Death Unknown

The story of Timothy Benson takes a slightly different turn to that of many of the highwaymen and women featured in this book. He was truly a man of conscience and a gentleman. Although he committed only one highway robbery, it affected him deeply.

Timothy Benson was the son of a woman who was married to a sergeant in the Earl of Derby's regiment. She had also been having a long-standing love affair with one Captain Benson. The sergeant, whose name doesn't appear on record, died shortly after Timothy was born. The mother declared that it was highly likely that her son was the illegitimate child of the captain and, therefore, named him Benson. Captain Benson took the child as his own without too much demur and had him educated at grammar school. Benson did well at school and behaved himself beautifully. In fact, the boy did so well that the captain sent him on to university at Leyden in Holland where he did equally well.

Unfortunately, the captain died of pleurisy not long after Benson's return, leaving the entirety of his estate to a nephew. It is possible that as the boy had continued to prove himself such a good and hardworking young man, the captain may have been able to amend the will to leave the boy something, but this had not happened and Benson was left with nothing. His newly impoverished position didn't immediately prompt Benson to turn away from an honest life, however. He lived frugally and spent a lot of time with his books. He paid all his bills and became well known in local society, where, had he any forethought, he might have fallen in love with the daughter of a well-off family. Ultimately, his inability to do this was the breaking of him.

Instead, Benson fell in love with Jenny, a **mantua maker's** apprentice and the daughter of a chandler, with no fortune to inherit or dowry to be bestowed on her at the time of her marriage. Jenny reciprocated Benson's advances and they became intimately involved, living on his savings. When these funds had depleted Benson had to admit that he had nothing: no fortune, no inheritance waiting and no job. With his education he could surely have found work as a clerk or a school teacher, but this is not the route that he chose to take.

The couple moved into a house at Red Lion Fields, with only 1 crown left to pay the rent and buy food. In desperation, Benson gave Jenny a diamond ring to pawn. While he waited for her to return he gazed out the window and, seeing a gentleman taking a walk, a sudden brainwave came to him. Immediately, without any thought of the repercussions of his actions, he put on a coat and a brace of pistols, left the house and, disguising his voice, he confronted the man with, 'Deliver or you're a dead man.' The man gave him his purse and began to take off his rings, but Benson stopped him, saying that the purse was plenty. He then told him to turn his back and stay in that position for fifteen minutes. Back in their lodgings, Benson took stock of his haul and found that the purse held 70 guineas and two rings, which he didn't think had much value, and later buried in the garden. The purse he threw in the fire.

Unlike some of his contemporary colleagues, Benson didn't feel elated at the ease with which the robbery was performed. He was wracked with guilt and fear at being caught and hanged. To help him ignore these whisperings of his conscience, he went downstairs to his landlady's parlour, where he heard a number of voices. And who did he see when he entered? None other than the poor man he had just robbed. The landlady explained the situation and said that the gentleman needed a glass of water to steady his nerves. Benson took his leave to sit with the company, offer his condolences and hear the full story of the wicked robbery.

The gentleman had, as he usually did, been exercising on the green when he was suddenly approached by a man muffled in a great coat with his hat obscuring his face and voice. The thief had taken only the purse, which contained a largish sum of money and two rings, but he refused to take the man's own ring. For that, the gentleman thought a lot of his assailant, who was about the height of the landlady's lodger. The gentleman confessed to being extremely short-sighted and said he wouldn't know the face again if he did see it and besides, the robber had acted in such a courteous manner that he doubted he'd be able to take legal action against him.

Benson, not believing his good luck, became very affable with the gentleman and took a glass of wine with him. The pair was still drinking when Jenny arrived home, at which point the gentleman asked for a coach to be called to take him home. Benson offered to accompany him, and Jenny was ready to race upstairs and get his distinctive, great coat. Benson told her that he wouldn't need it, fearing recognition, and hastily ushered the guest out of the house and saw him to his door.

On his return, Jenny told Benson that she could only get 3 guineas for the ring. He didn't seem too worried by this small amount and said that things were bound to get better. He then pretended that Captain Benson's nephew had urged him to take 20 guineas as part of an inheritance that he should have had. Jenny didn't see any reason to disbelieve Tim's story and they were comfortable for a while.

Although his first robbery had been easy, Benson didn't want to go down the road of highway robbery to make his living. Finally, he decided to set up as a quack doctor to draw on some of the science that he had learnt as a youth. The couple then moved to Huntingdon to start this new enterprise. Jenny stayed in their lodgings while Benson travelled the country selling his drugs. It proved to be quite a profitable little profession and they made about £500 over the next three years.

It was when he returned to London to try his luck selling his wares in the city that it looked as though the whole scheme would fall through and he'd end up at the end of the hangman's rope. Benson was arrested on suspicion of committing a robbery of 7 guineas, a **snuff box** and a silver watch. He waited in gaol until his trial came up, but the evidence didn't hold against him and finally another inmate of the prison confessed to the theft and even produced the stolen goods. Benson was acquitted, but he was shaken by the experience as his conscience was still pricking him over his first and only robbery.

Following this scare, the couple resolved to make a new life for themselves in America. But, before they could do this, Benson set off to London to right the wrong he had done when they first set up house together. He wrote a letter to the injured man and enclosed £100 for the 70 guineas that he had taken in the purse and to compensate for the stolen rings, which he admitted he had sold later on. He ended by asking the old man's pardon.

Timothy Benson's story has a happy ending. He and Jenny travelled across the ocean and set up business in the plantations in America. He did so well that he was able to retire as a gentleman and live the life that he was never born to have.

WILLIAM BEW

Birthdate Unknown • Died 1689

William Bew was the brother of another notorious highwayman, Captain Bew, who was killed in the process of being apprehended at Knightsbridge. It is thought that William was probably as great a villain as his brother. I have included Bew in this anthology of highway robbers because of a funny little anecdote concerning one of his robberies. We have heard so much about gallant highwaymen, dashing in a froth of lace and velvet, offering courtesy and flirtations to pretty ladies; this story offers a new dimension to that ideal.

William was out one day, going about his business of robbing people on the highway, when he happened upon a young woman on horseback accompanied by a solitary servant. William rode up and began flattering the woman, telling her of her exceptional beauty. Enjoying the attentions of this rather handsome young man, she joined in by telling him he was wrong; it was all nonsense and she was nothing of the sort. The woman was obviously courting more flattery rather than trying to shut her companion up.

When the road was quiet of any other travellers, William stopped the party and told her that it was actually the beauty of her money and valuables that he'd been discussing, not her beauty, and that he'd have those things from her straightaway!

MARY BLACKET (ALIAS FRANCES)

Born *c*. 1692 • Died *c*. 1726

Mary Blacket was another victim of poverty and perhaps of a deep injustice as well. Her parents were very poor, but still found means of giving their daughter an education. She learnt to read and write, sew and do other things that she might need to do as a domestic servant.

When Blacket became an adult, she got a position in a household and lived there very well until she met the man she was to marry. He was a sailor and often at sea. Everyone who knew her thought that she worked honestly while he was away. It is, therefore, easy to imagine the surprise of those around her when she was arrested and taken to Newgate on suspicion of robbing and assaulting William Whittle on the highway on 6 August 1726.

Throughout her incarceration and at her trial, Blacket insisted that she was innocent of the crime, but the jury found her guilty and she was given a death sentence. Blacket's biggest fear was for her daughter's welfare when she was dead.

The fact that Mary insisted on her innocence throughout her ordeal, and that her neighbours and friends were ignorant of her criminal activities, makes the modern reader wonder if this wasn't a case of mistaken identity or some other error that led an innocent woman to hang at Tyburn.

JOSEPH BLAKE (ALIAS BLUESKIN)

Born 1700 • Died 1724

Joseph Blake was a Londoner by birth and his parents, Nathaniel and Jane Blake, were financially stable enough to have their son educated at the parish school of St Giles-without-Cripplegate for six years. His main influence at school was that of a fellow school mate, William Blewitt, who enjoyed all sorts of mischief and was more than happy to drag Blake along with him. It was Blewitt who introduced Blake to the criminal fraternity and its boss, Jonathon Wild.

Blake embarked on an apprenticeship as a pickpocket for Wild's gang and, after leaving school, he was set to make his fortune as a robber. He had no intention of trying any legal employment; this was his sole ambition. He was all of 17 and was already using his nickname 'Blueskin'. How he earned this moniker is a matter of speculation. One suggestion is that he had a port wine birthmark, another that he had a lot of facial hair or that he had a swarthy complexion. There was even the idea that he took it from the surname of his friend Blewitt.

Blake joined the well-known Carrick gang, which consisted of Irishman James Carrick, Lock, Robert Wilkinson, Lincoln and Daniel Carrol. Under their guidance, the youth committed a number of highway robberies and other crimes. In fact, there wasn't a type of crime that they didn't commit, though they were not always successful. For example, they once tried to rob a soldier, but he was a captain who handled his pistol so well that the thieves were unable to take anything from him.

Blake hadn't been with the gang long when Robert Wilkinson was caught and arrested. Wilkinson, in an attempt to save his own skin, handed over the names of many of his comrades, including that of Blake. Several were arrested on account of the information; three were later hanged because of it. Blake received a nasty cut to the head when he tried to resist arrest.

When Blake was taken into custody he took Wilkinson's lack of loyalty as his own model and admitted evidence against certain members of the gang. He told the court that they had made more than seventy robberies and that they had also murdered a Chelsea Pensioner, Peter Martin. He also gave evidence of a robbery with violence made against a man in Fig Lane who was badly bashed about the head when he was slow in giving in to their demands. The beating they gave him was so severe that it was lucky that he didn't die of his injuries. On Blake's evidence, the perpetrators of this crime were arrested, tried and subsequently executed.

Jonathon Wild used his influence to have Blake's sentence reduced from death to transportation. Blake refused to be transported, but was eventually released from prison when a couple of people vouched for his good behaviour. As he walked out of the gate, somebody asked him how long it would be before they saw him again at the Old Bailey. One gentleman suggested that it would be in three session's time, which proved to be accurate.

Carrick himself and at least twenty members of his gang (including Blake) were taken by Jonathon Wild's men in the August of 1724. Carrick was hanged for a theft that Wild later had another man executed for.

Once out of gaol, Blake immediately found himself a new partner in crime: Jack Sheppard, a notorious house-breaker. The two committed several heinous crimes, including the robbery and assault of a man called Pargiter. Blake hit him and he fell unconscious into a muddy ditch. He would have drowned if Sheppard hadn't come to his aid and held his face out of the water. The crime was blamed on two brothers called Brightwell, who would have been found guilty of the assault had they not had staunch witnesses to provide them both with alibis. One of the brothers died a week after being released from gaol. Although he had been cleared of the crime, he didn't live to hear Blake's full confession of it.

It was during this brief time of freedom that Blake, with Sheppard, worked the Hampstead Road, holding up all and sundry. Their behaviour had nothing romantic or gentlemanly about it; the two were brutal and without conscience.

After one of their next house-breaking adventures, when they tried to pass stolen goods to one of Wild's own fences, Wild tracked down Sheppard (for whom he held a deep grudge) at Blake's mother's wine shop in Rosemary Lane (near the Tower of London) and arrested him. It was not easy to keep Sheppard behind bars and he escaped within hours of his capture. A month later, Wild had Sheppard locked up again; this time with his wife. They both escaped a few days later.

While Sheppard was on the run yet again, Blake had been tracked down by Wild for his part in the robbery of the house belonging to Mr Kneebone (who was actually a former employer of Sheppard). Blake and Sheppard (who was in custody once more, and this time shackled to the floor of his cell in Newgate prison) were found guilty of the crime and sentenced to hang. The evidence of Blake's part in the robbery was given by Wild and his men. The account differed dramatically from that which they gave at Shepherd's trial for the same offence, but Blake was still found guilty.

Blake tried to persuade Wild to speak on his behalf and have the sentence reduced to transportation, as he had once before, but Wild refused. Blake lashed out at him with a weapon he had concealed about him and slashed Wild's throat. A surgeon was called for and Wild's life was saved. During the commotion, however, Sheppard managed to escape, taking his chain and shackles with him. Blake also attempted a break out from the prison, but he wasn't successful.

Joseph Blake remained defiant while awaiting his execution and declared (to anyone who could be bothered to listen) that he wished he'd had the means to cut Wild's head off. It wasn't

Blake's attack on Jonathon Wild.

until the morning of his execution that he showed any sign of remorse at all, and that was likely only because his impending death frightened him.

Blake left the world with no friends to mourn him. He had been a ruthless criminal and disloyal to his own gang. He was hanged on 11 November 1724 and he was buried in St Andrew's churchyard in Holborn.

Blake's reputation was built on his associations with larger criminals, such as James Carrick and Jack Sheppard, and also for his outrageously brave attack on the self-styled Thief-Taker General, Jonathon Wild, who was the biggest crook of them all. There is, however, little recorded about his actual acts of highway robbery.

NED BONNET

Birthdate Unknown • Died 1713

Edward 'Ned' Bonnet began his adult life as a law-abiding grocer. He came from a reputable family in the Isle of Ely, Cambridgeshire, and received a modest education. He was a successful businessman, even a wealthy one, worth over £600 at one stage, until misfortune struck. A savage fire destroyed both his business and home, and Bonnet was left destitute. He fled from his debtors straight into a gang of highwaymen and they embraced him like a long-lost brother.

Bonnet's original plan was to make enough money from highway robbery to set himself up in business again. However, the trade of robbery proved far too lucrative and enjoyable and he decided to make it a permanent career change. He is purported to have performed over 300 robberies.

Bonnet carried on his new trade undaunted by further misfortune. When his horse was shot and killed during one robbery, he continued to hold up travellers without his trusty steed until he was able to steal another from the innkeeper of the Red Lion in Hounslow.

Shortly afterwards, Bonnet was riding along the highway towards Cambridgeshire, humming, of all things, a psalm, which, whether it was part of his plan or not, meant that a fellow traveller riding up beside him thought that he was a God-fearing man and, therefore, trustworthy. They travelled together for some time until they were on a lonely stretch of road. Suddenly, Bonnet turned to his new friend and ordered him to 'Stand and deliver!'.

It was a good haul, over 80 guineas. Bonnet, feeling a touch magnanimous in his good fortune, gave his victim a half-crown to keep him going until he was able to re-make his fortune. Perhaps a fit of nostalgia overtook him and he remembered his own time as a prosperous grocer, cut short in his prime. Little acts of mercy such as this were what gave highwaymen their reputation of being gentlemen.

The victim may have been relieved that he wasn't killed outright, but he was probably hardly disposed to thank his robber for his thoughtfulness. Apparently, he couldn't stand hearing psalms sung after his episode on the road.

Ned Bonnet's downfall came when a fellow highwayman, Zachary Clare, reported him to the authorities in a plea to save his own skin.

The former grocer and former upstanding citizen was executed on Saturday 28 March 1713.

EDWARD AND JOAN BRACEY

Edward: Birthdate Unknown • Died 1685
Joan: Born *c.* 1656 • Died 1685

There is no record of an official marriage between this pair of highway robbers, but Joan certainly took Bracey's name as her own. They met when Edward tried to swindle Joan's father out of a large sum of money; he was a wealthy farmer and Edward's plan was to make love to the daughter, marry her for her dowry and rob the father of anything else he could get, after which he would ditch the daughter and flee. Edward, however, met his match in Joan, who discovered his plan and (perhaps barring the marriage bit) helped him rob her father and fled with him. The two were inseparable and built their life together by robbing on the highway and in the street, from shoplifting to pickpocketing.

Even though they set about their business with bravado and enjoyment, the fear of getting caught and hanged was always with them and when they had amassed a small fortune, they decided to give up the criminal life and establish a legitimate business.

Edward and Joan set up an inn on the outskirts of Bristol that did a very good trade. Joan was very attractive and let the young male customers declare their love for her and then spend all their money on drink. As far as it is known, she didn't go further than this kind of encouragement, except when it was a plan hatched between her and her partner to fleece someone.

A Mr Day was one such victim. Joan had promised him a night of passion with her while her husband was away. A maid let Mr Day in and said that her mistress was waiting for him in her bedroom. She told the man that he was to strip off right there and then before she could show him up to her mistress. This was, the maid explained, because there may be the necessity to run out of the bedroom in a hurry, get dressed in secret and leave without detection. The maid left the room while the man got undressed. He was then led to the door of what he believed to be Joan's room. Instead, the door led to a back alley that was little more than an open sewer. When he realised that he'd been tricked, Mr Day made his way home as quickly as he could in the dark before he could be discovered and publicly humiliated.

There were other tricks similarly played on guests of the inn and it rapidly gained a bad reputation. In fact, before they had had it for a year, they had to shut up shop and return to their more successful employment of highway robbery.

Not only did they rob travellers (with Joan often dressed as a man), but the couple used their knowledge of former clients of their inn to extort money, even if it was owed to them as a debt racked up by the customer. Joan was often the brains behind this kind of operation.

In 1685, when Joan was about 29, she was caught during a hold-up on a coach and taken to Nottingham gaol. She was tried, sentenced and executed in April of that year.

Edward Bracey escaped when his wife was captured and went into hiding. He was nearly caught at an inn a little while later. When the soldiers arrived, having been given a tip-off, Edward pretended that he was a serving man employed at the inn and offered them his assistance. He quit the room, mounted his horse and raced off, leaving a couple of his then gang members to be arrested.

Edward Bracey met his end only a few days after this when his horse, tethered at a doorway, was recognised by a victim of the Braceys'. The guards were called and Edward, hearing the commotion, attempted to mount his horse and ride off, but the horse was shot from under him and he received several gunshot wounds to his body. Edward Bracey died from his injuries three days later.

MARY BRYANT

Born 1765 • Date of Death Unknown

Mary Bryant is well known, not because of her criminal activity, but for her punishment.

She was born to William Broad, fisherman, and his wife, Grace Symons, in Fowey, Cornwall. As a youth, she left home for Plymouth in England, expecting to find work there. Mary found employment, but probably not what she had anticipated. She became apprenticed to a gang of thieves and became quite proficient at petty theft. Yet she was not skilful enough to avoid being caught. Her last crime was to commit a highway robbery with a couple of friends, taking a silk bonnet, some money and jewellery. As it was her first offence and she was pregnant, she was handed down a sentence of seven years' transportation to Australia. This was the event that really made her name. She was one of the first convicts sent to Australia on the First Fleet in 1788.

She gave birth to a girl, whom she called Charlotte (named after the ship on which they were sailing) and gave the child the surname Spence, which is thought be based on the surname of the possible father, another prisoner, David Spencer. It was not Spencer, however, that she married when they landed in Sydney Cove, but a fellow deportee, William Bryant from Cornwall, who had been a smuggler. Their son, Emmanuel, was born in 1790.

Life was hard in the new colony and William, given a job with responsibility, looking after the fishing boats, broke the trust of his masters by selling fish to convicts. He was given 100 lashes for the offence. After this, William planned to escape from the barbaric place with his wife and children.

In 1791, the small family and a crew of seven men set sail in a small boat. The boat was insufficient for the purpose of such a long journey, yet in sixty-six days they travelled 5,000km and reached Kupang in Timor.

At the time, Timor was under Dutch rule. The Bryants pretended to be shipwreck survivors, but were found to be convicts from Britain when William drunkenly spilled the beans. They were sent back to Britain to stand trial for having broken their bond of seven years' hard labour in Australia.

The voyage, notoriously dangerous, uncomfortable and unhealthy, proved fatal for William and the two children. Mary arrived back in England six years after she had left it. She was expecting a death sentence or to be returned to Australia. In the end, neither of these occurred. She was made to stay for a year in Newgate and then her cause, taken up by James Boswell, was made public and she was granted a full pardon in 1793. Boswell provided her with an annuity of £10 for the rest of her life. What she did with it and when and where she died is unknown. Hopefully, she was able to settle down to a new life with a new husband and new children, not a replacement for the past, but perhaps some solace for it.

All for the sake of a petty theft, an unknown and otherwise unremarkable young woman became a folk hero who inspired songs, plays, novels and musicals about her extraordinary voyage from Australia, across an uncharted reef to an island in the Pacific in a small boat.

Mary Bryant.

WILLIAM BURK

Born 1700 • Died 1723

William Burk was born in St Catherine's in the vicinity of the Tower of London. When he was 11 he ran away after receiving a severe punishment from the master at the parish charity school. Burk ran straight to the harbour and boarded a ship bound for Jamaica, *The Salisbury*. When William's mother tracked him down and pleaded with him to come home, the boy used the captain's influence as master of the ship to refuse her request and so he set sail as a cabin boy.

During the voyage, *The Salisbury* encountered a Spanish galleon, which they challenged to battle, with the victor taking the other ship's entire store as booty. Burk was injured in the fight, but they were victorious. Before they reached port, another galleon was taken and the reward for *The Salisbury*'s crew members amounted to approximately £15 each and significantly more for the officers.

Once in Jamaica, Burk was approached by an English woman and offered employment in her inn. At first, he was a willing and able employee, but at some point he attempted to defraud his mistress. When he was caught he humbly begged for forgiveness. The woman let all charges drop, but did not reinstate him in her employ.

Burk then went back to a sailor's life and experienced several near-misses on his life, including one in which some of the crew were killed by the indigenous population of Guinea. Burk's next major voyage was on a man-of-war going north into the Baltic. The cold was so bad that it put him off sailing for the rest of his life.

The trip back home to England was also very bad. Food was in such short supply that the rations for each man were about two spoonfuls a day for much of the trip, and towards the end two spoonfuls were to last them five days. When he returned to England, Burk turned his back on his sailing life and became a highwayman instead. His main focus was on robbing travellers on the road around Stepney. The only thing really known about Burk's activities as a highwayman is that his weapon of choice was not a pistol, but a hedge bill. He threatened his victims with this nasty piece of equipment and even went as far as to hit an old man he had attempted to rob.

Having been a fine sailor and a brave one, Burk did not make a successful highwayman. He was arrested for holding up and robbing William Fitzer, which was only his third or fourth hold-up. At the Old Bailey, he was also charged with a similar offence against James Westwood, which he had committed on the same day as the Fitzer robbery.

When he knew that his fate was sealed, William Burk became remorseful and turned to God for solace. He was hanged at Tyburn on 8 April 1723.

WILLIAM BURRIDGE

Born *c.* 1688 • Died 1722

William Burridge's father was a carpenter from West Haden in Northamptonshire. The boy learnt reading, writing and arithmetic and was destined to become apprenticed to his father. Burridge, however, did not like this and often ran away to find more entertaining ways to spend his days. He enjoyed wrestling and cudgel playing and often performed feats in these sports at local fairs, where there were cash prizes for the winners.

Burridge's father was disappointed in his son's attitude to the trade that he was supposed to be working in and finally found another master craftsman to take the boy on. This didn't work either, and William paid even less attention to his legitimate work than ever. Apparently, he was a great favourite amongst the local servant girls and would seek out their company whenever possible. Burridge was said to be a handsome young man.

Burridge's apprenticeship with his new master did not last and the boy was dismissed well before his time was served. When he returned home, he found a rather cool reception waiting for him from his family. Unimpressed by his irresponsible antics and lack of serious application to his trade, they suggested that he join the navy. This was a step that appealed to William, as it did to other restless youths, and he set sail for Spain on a ship under the command of Commodore Cavendish. Fighting was something at which Burridge excelled and he was certainly brave. During a battle in the Bay of Cadiz he fought so well that he received a number of high commendations. Unfortunately, praise made Burridge arrogant and he was no longer happy to take orders from senior officers. The outcome of this was that the men who could have helped him to make a real name for himself in the navy refused to have anything to do with him.

When there was no more fighting to be done, Burridge returned to England and tried to find employment. He didn't want a menial or boring job and he didn't want to labour for someone else. It was much more attractive to be self-sufficient by robbing people on the road. His ambition was to make a decent amount of money on which he could retire and not have to even make the effort of robbing coaches.

Burridge's career as a highwayman probably shows a true and unromantic picture of what it was like from the criminal's point of view. There are many tales of how the thieves stole hundreds and thousands of pounds from wealthy travellers, which they then spent rapidly on alcohol and women (or men). Burridge found that he couldn't make the crime pay enough for the risks that he ran and the constant evasion of the law. He was also a regular inmate of Bridewell for his participation in public brawls; it seemed that he could never resist the temptation to have a fist fight.

Burridge escaped once from New Prison with the aid of a woman, and escaped hanging at a later time when he gave evidence against another robber called Reading, who was in turn tried and hanged for the crime.

After a long and not very successful career as a highway robber, William Burridge was caught stealing a horse and was taken to and tried at the Old Bailey, and sentenced to death. After hearing his sentence Burridge was full of remorse for the crimes he had committed. At the age of 34 he was one of the older highwaymen to be hanged. He was executed at Tyburn on 14 March 1722.

JAMES BUTLER

Birthdate Unknown • Died 1723

James Butler was apprenticed to a silversmith at great expense to his father, who had a very modest income. It was, therefore, all the more ungrateful of him to run away from his master after only six months of indenture, but he had the urge to go to sea on a fighting ship.

As a cabin boy waiting on the captain, Butler did very well for himself and received encouragements and rewards for his service, even though it was known that James was a petty thief. He was given plenty of warnings from the captain, but he refused to heed them. The last straw came when Butler was caught poking his nose into a crewman's chest. He was reported to the captain who said that, despite all the kindness and indulgences he had made to the boy, it had not stopped his thieving ways. He was, therefore, obliged to dismiss Butler from his crew when they returned to England. Butler was then given 2 guineas to help him make his way back on shore. The hope was that he would go home to his parents, but this was not to be. Instead, he worked on board several other ships. He continued his sneakiness and thievery and eventually gained such a bad reputation that no ship would have him. His last ship was the *Mary* and he was dismissed from service on it in 1721.

Back on land, Butler took little time in getting acquainted with a gang of highway robbers whose territory lay on the road between Buckingham House and Chelsea. His gang comprised the notorious robbers Dyer, Duce and Rice.

The dangers of highway robbery hit home for Butler after an incident in which the gang attempted to hold up a coach on 27 April 1723. Joseph Rice was shot dead by one of the footmen. Butler decided that he'd try another form of employment after witnessing the death of his colleague. He left the gang a few days after Rice's death and began to work honestly as a labourer for a man called Cladins in Wandsworth, Surrey. It was too late, though; Butler's name had been given along with other members of the gang and his wife had been taken to Bridewell to tell of her husband's current whereabouts. Butler, rather than be arrested, took to the road again.

His new gang members consisted of Wade, Meads, Garns and Spigget, who worked the Gravesend Road. These robbers were not averse to violence by any means and during a couple of robberies they deliberately shot a footman in order to instil as much fear as possible into the passengers. During another robbery the gang wounded one of their victims, put him on a horse and told him to ride to Gravesend. The frightened, injured man disobeyed and rode off in a different direction. When Meads saw this he chased after him and shot him at point blank range in the face, killing him instantly.

The law got Butler eventually and he was tried and sentenced to death for his part in the crimes committed by his gang, to which he openly confessed, although there seems to have been some doubt as to whether he really did everything he claimed to have done.

JAMES CARRICK (ALIAS VALENTINE)

Born *c.* 1695 • Died 1722

James Carrick was born the youngest child to a gentleman's family with an estate near Dublin. Carrick, like the rest of his siblings, received a fair education and was destined by his father to become an **ensign**.

Carrick went with his regiment to Spain and used the large amount of money his father had given him for living expenses on luxuries. While stationed in Barcelona, he got involved in a number of intrigues, frauds and petty thefts. The success of these gave him the confidence to carry on in a similar vein when he returned with his regiment to England.

Carrick then took up with two men, Smith and Butler (not the James Butler listed elsewhere in this book), and they became a small gang of highwaymen. The trio were soon caught, but Carrick's life was spared because of the evidence he gave against his gang. The other two members were hanged.

Carrick's brother in Ireland despaired of his new career and bade him to come home on his release from prison, where he would be provided for by the family. Carrick had no intention of taking up the generous offer of his brother and went straight back on the highway, robbing on Finchley Common, Hounslow Heath and Bagshot Heath with a renewed sense of enthusiasm.

Carrick loved fashionable clothes, pretty girls and gambling, and was able to spend all his stolen money in a very short amount of time. Every time he was obliged to go on the highway to fill his dwindling coffers added a greater risk of getting caught.

By this time, Carrick had got together another little gang, comprising of John Molony and Daniel Carrol, all Irishmen like himself. They not only committed highway robbery, but took to robbing on the streets of the city as well. This gang was equally ill-fated and Molony and Carrick were caught soon after they attempted to rob the Honourable William Young Esquire in his sedan chair. Carrol was able to get out of England and went into hiding in Ireland, where he turned to street robbery. He was later killed during an arrest attempt in Dublin.

Carrick was detained at Newgate and entertained a large numbers of visitors, all eager to hear of his adventures. During his time as a thief, highwayman and general criminal, Carrick was involved with a number of other highwaymen (all mentioned in this book): Humphrey Angier, Joseph 'Blueskin' Blake, Robert Wilkinson and John Molony. The keepers at the prison charged a fee for the public to go in and listen to Carrick's tales of them.

On 18 July 1722, Carrick put the noose about his own neck while he was on the scaffold and was hanged without protest.

WILLIAM COLTHOUSE

Born *c*. 1688 • Died 1722

William Colthouse was born in Yorkshire to poor parents who, despite their low income, managed to give their son a decent education with a strong emphasis on religion. As a young man he got involved in political beliefs that went against the grain of those that were in government at the time (under King George I). He declared these beliefs openly and was imprisoned in Newgate on a charge of sedition. For Colthouse, Newgate was the worst place he could have ended up. As with so many easily influenced youngsters, he made the wrong sort of acquaintances.

After he was released from prison, he and his brother decided to try their hand at highway robbery. At first, they were quite successful, making a handsome living for the two of them. Things went wrong, however, during one particular robbery on Hounslow Heath. William's brother was captured while Colthouse managed to hide from his pursuers in a hollow tree. His brother was duly tried and executed.

Being severely shaken by his brother's death, Colthouse became a chastened man and swore he'd never rob again. He became a journeyman joiner in Oxford. Yet turning away from crime was easier said than done, and as the arduousness of work took its toll, so too did his determination to be good. After a while, he threw in his work and went to London to find easier pickings.

As a **Jacobite** only too willing to voice his opinions, Colthouse found himself in trouble at an inn in Tothill Fields in Westminster. He'd been drinking at the inn when he said something derogatory about the prince, which was overheard by a group soldiers. The men grabbed hold of him and threw him onto the gridiron (grill). The burn made a deep scar under his left eye. It was this scar that was to be the deciding factor in his arrest soon after for the murder of a boy in Hampshire. Colthouse loudly protested his innocence, which was supported by the fact that there was no other evidence to link him to it. Still, in this case, justice did not prevail and William Colthouse was found guilty and sentenced to hang.

The condemned man wrote a letter to two of his surviving brothers, exhorting them to stay on the right side of the law. It had come to his ears that the pair was practising highway robbery. Of the younger brother, he refused to believe it, but he wasn't quite so sure of the other one.

Colthouse was joined in Newgate by another pair of infamous highwaymen, John Smith (alias Shaw) and Jonah Burgess. The three planned a means of escape using pistols that they had been able to get smuggled in to them. Before they could put their plan into action, however, it was discovered by the authorities and thwarted. Jonah Burgess slashed his own throat, although not fatally, and said that Smith had been going to use the pistols to shoot himself rather than hang. Smith refused to corroborate this story and berated Burgess for thinking of suicide as a suitable end. Smith declared that it would only give their enemies double satisfaction for not only having them dead, but for knowing that their souls were damned as well.

Colthouse denied any part in the plan until the day of his execution and then he confessed to having been involved in it and admitted that it was he who had arranged to have the pistols brought into prison. Colthouse was hanged at Tyburn on 8 February 1722, along with John Smith and Jonah Burgess.

LUMLEY DAVIS

Birthdate Unknown • Date of Death Unknown

Lumley Davis was the son of Lumley Davis Senior, who was wealthy enough to have all of his sons educated in one of the best schools in England. Davis Junior was an outstanding student academically and the school would have taken him on as a teacher. It seems that Davis had other ideas, however, as to the surprise of all his family and friends he got an apprenticeship with a vintner instead.

Although this was his own choice, it was not to the boy's liking either, and it wasn't long before he threw in his apprenticeship and ran up huge debts. For this, he was arrested and taken to the Marshalsea. It was in the debtors' prison that, amongst others, he made friends with John Harman (see his entry later in the book). How long he would have languished in the gaol is up for speculation had a friend not come to his rescue, paid all his debts and his prison fine, so that Davis could be set free.

When released and left to his own devices, Davis took himself straight to an alehouse and began drinking. Yet his continued life of debauchery took a heavy toll on his health and he fell ill. At this point, the same friend that had bailed him out of the Marshalsea took him to St Thomas' Hospital, taking care of all the medical bills. When Davis was ready to leave the hospital, his friend supplied him with a country retreat for his recuperation. The friend also made sure that Davis was supplied with books to keep his mind occupied, and perhaps in the hope that the young man would do something constructive with his life.

If this was the plan, it didn't work. Once recovered, Davis quickly got bored and left the quiet country life for the delights of London. One of his quests, besides enjoying himself, was to hunt down one of his new acquaintances from the Marshalsea, a Mr Harman, and begin a career as a highwayman. Unfortunately, neither of the gentlemen were particularly adept at the craft and the first haul they made was when they robbed John Nichols, Esq. They managed to only take 1 guinea 17s. It was hardly a princely sum, but enough to tide them over, and they felt that it was too dangerous to go out again so soon. But even if they had wanted to resume their new occupation, their luck was out because their very first robbery was also their last. They were arrested, tried and found guilty. The sentence for each was death.

Davis didn't think that the sentence would be carried out. In the past, someone had always come to his aid, but this time there was nothing anyone could do. At the last minute, he applied himself to his Bible in the hope of saving his soul. He also tried to speak as often as he could with his friend Harman and those who were also destined to hang for their crimes. Davis, who could have had a long and profitable life, was hanged at the age of 23.

SIR GOSSELIN DENVILLE

Birthdate Unknown • Date of Death Unknown
Lived in the time of King Edward II

Sir Gosselin Denville, as his name suggests, was descended from a knight who served William the Conqueror. The knight was given land in Yorkshire in the town of Northallerton and turned it into a wealthy estate for his heirs down the generations.

Denville was sent to Peter College, Cambridge and was destined for the priesthood by his father. The son, it seems, had other ideas and on discovering the future chosen for him began a steady rebellion against it.

When Denville's father died, he (as the eldest son) inherited the entire estate along with an annual income of £1,200. It didn't take Denville and his brother Robert long to get through their money and to ruin the estate, and there was nothing left to do but form a gang and turn to the king's highway for their living.

Their first known victims were a pair of cardinals sent by the Pope in Rome to help broker peace between England and Scotland, King Edward II and the Earl of Lancaster. The sharing of the large haul taken from the cardinals caused a major rift between the Denville brothers and one of their men, a man called Middleton, which resulted in Middleton leaving the gang to rob on his own. He was soon caught, tried and hanged.

Denville's gang grew in numbers and strength, so much so that they were every traveller's nightmare. The gang forged a reputation for ruthlessness and violence often ending in murder. The gang, however, could also act completely out of character and let their victims go intact with goods and life. One such case was recorded when they held up a Dominican monk, Andrew Sympson, who was ordered to sit in a tree and

give them a sermon. His performance was so good that he
was allowed to go home with his money.

The mercy of the act of letting Sympson go was more to do
with the whims of the Denvilles than any real feeling towards
the man. The gang continued their reign of terror on the road
and had scores of soldiers out trying to catch them and bring
them before the courts. The biggest event of Denville's career
is his supposed hold-up of King Edward II himself. The story
has never been verified as true, but such a daring attempt by
a bandit like Denville is highly possible. The gang, kitted out
as priests, met the king on the road near Norwich. The king
stopped out of respect for the religious group and was happy
for Denville to come and talk to him.

Gosselin bowed and then politely told His Majesty the true
nature of himself and his men, offering a threat to the king
in very polite language, unless all money and valuables were
handed over. No one escaped a personalised search through
bags and pockets.

*King Edward II about to meet
Denville on the road.*

A high price was put on the head of Denville and any member of his gang, alive or dead. A great many of them were subsequently captured and put to trial. Denville and one of his brothers continued to terrorise the countryside with even more viciousness than before. Apparently, wealthy citizens refused to travel to their country estates during these times for fear of the gang.

The last recorded robbery by the gang took place in the north of England at the residence of the Bishop of Durham. After binding and gagging the bishop and his staff, they ransacked the palace, drank as much wine as they could in the cellar and let the rest run out of the casks. Before they left, Denville told the bishop to call on God for help.

Perhaps God felt that this was the last straw or Denville became too complacent in his powers to evade the law, for after the attack on the Bishop of Durham, he was finally apprehended.

He had been a keen customer of an inn in Yorkshire, mainly because he was having an openly amorous affair with the publican's wife. For some time, the innkeeper had put up with Denville cuckolding him; after all, the highwayman's presence guaranteed a healthy income. Yet even money can lose its attraction and so it did for the innkeeper who was sick of being the butt of jokes about his wife and Denville.

The county sheriff was delighted to be tipped off as to the current whereabouts of Denville and his gang, and it is said that he took 500 or 600 soldiers with him to take the men. It is also reported that Denville's gang killed a third of them before the highwayman finally had to surrender.

The gang was taken to York where they were publicly executed, without trial, before a large audience.

SAWNEY DOUGLAS

Born 1611 • Died 1664

Sawney Douglas was born in Portpatrick in Galloway, Scotland in 1611. His father was a tanner. Little is known of his life prior to the outbreak of the English Civil War in 1641. Sawney was a Parliamentarian and against the king. He participated in the Battle of Dundee where, he claimed, he killed twenty-nine men. It was to be the beginning of a blood-thirsty career.

By the time the English monarchy was restored in the form of Charles II, Douglas had been a soldier for twenty years or more. As a member of the opposition, he was no longer able to be employed as such and had to look for employment in another field. Douglas chose highway robbery, not unlike many other Civil War survivors from either side.

He got himself a horse by lying in wait beside the road until a suitable mount appeared. A man servant finally obliged, complete with a brace of pistols, and Douglas engaged him in light conversation until an opportunity came for him to knock the man off his horse and bash him senseless. Leaving the servant unconscious in a ditch, Douglas took the horse and rode off.

Meaning to go on as he had started, Douglas was in no way a gentlemen robber, but one who was totally self-centred and ruthless. The first robbery recorded after taking the horse was made at Maidenhead Thicket in Berkshire where he held up the Mayor of Thornbury, Gloucestershire, Mr Thurston. From this man, he took £18 and refused the victim's plea to be left enough to get himself home again. The Duchess of Albemarle was another victim, whom he divested of several items of valuable jewellery.

With the proceeds of these and other robberies, Douglas found accommodation with a well-to-do apothecary and his wealthy daughter in Westminster. The girl had a fortune of £2,000. Both father and daughter thought that Douglas was indeed the gentlemen he purported to be and they encouraged his advances.

Unfortunately for Douglas, but fortunately for the girl involved, the robber's money ran out and he was exposed as the rogue he truly was and evicted from their home. It was then back to the highway, where Douglas became friends with the legendary Claude Duval, which seems an unlikely match when the former was regarded as a cruel rogue and the other was a charming and polite gentlemen, although a robber.

It was while trying to rob the Earl of Sandwich that Douglas's career came to a sudden end. The earl was a noted soldier and was not going to let some grubby thief make him 'Stand and deliver!'. He was armed and shot Douglas's horse from under him. Stunned by the shock, Douglas was easily apprehended by the earl's servants, bound and taken to Newgate and then Tyburn.

Douglas was another unrepentant, openly defiant highwayman who went to his death without tears, prayers or duplications. He told the crowd that he should be able to hang in peace and he took a copy of *The Ballad of Chevy Chase* to the gallows with him instead of the usual bible. He then ordered the hangman be quick doing his job.

Sawney Douglas was hanged at Tyburn on 10 September 1664 at the age of 53.

JOHN DOYLE

Birthdate Unknown • Died 1730

The history of John Doyle was written down by the ordinary at Newgate prison to Doyle's dictation and shows the man to be an honest thief, only robbing when there was a possibility of the county paying the victim back and often leaving the victim with money in hand to get home. He also never used violence. As the words come from the criminal's own lips, there may be speculation as to their truthfulness.

John Doyle was an Irishman from Carrough. He was taught the basics of reading and writing, keeping accounts and some Latin. With these skills, he was apprenticed to a tallow-chandler and soap-boiler in Dublin. He served his full apprenticeship of seven years and then worked another nine months as a journeyman for the same master. After this, Doyle told his family that he wanted to set up his own business and they gave him £50 to help him do this. It was a ruse to get easy money and Doyle had no intention of working for his living at all.

In 1715, when the £50 was just about gone, Doyle made his way to England and immediately became a highwayman. For his new position, he used the last of his money to buy a pair of pistols in West Chester for 40s.

He prepared himself for his first hold-up while waiting for the Chester coach to leave for London. When it had got about 4 miles out of town, Doyle stopped it and took from the passengers £14 6s 9d, plus two silver watches and a mourning ring. Not a bad haul for his first attempt.

Having made his first wage packet, so to speak, John Doyle used it to purchase a horse in Shrewsbury. A former highwayman, making a career change, sold him one for 7s. Perhaps the robber wanted to unload the horse quickly because it could be recognised by a witness, or perhaps he just needed ready cash, because it was worth nearly three times that amount.

The first robbery that Doyle made with his new mount was on a chaise containing a couple of ladies and their single servant. Doyle's horse had been well trained and was able to take its new master right up to the door of the coach without hesitation. The ladies handed over 29½s and two gold watches. The servant was also made to hand over his pistols.

Doyle appears to have robbed only when he needed money, not for the actual fun of it, because after this second robbery he took a break in Newbury, Berkshire, keeping a low profile for the entire time that he was there. When the Newbury coach left for London, however, Doyle set out after it and overtook it when it was 5 miles out of the town. His professional highwayman's horse took him directly to the coach door again when bid and his master, in a professional highwayman's manner, asked the passengers to hand over their goods. There was no attempt at bravado or reluctance to comply; the haul amounted to £29, a silver watch, a gold wedding ring, a **snuff box** and a whip. One of the travellers was upset at handing over a ring with great family value and took the step of asking if he could have it back. Doyle handed it back over and the grateful man said he would never bear witness in court against Doyle. Not only did he promise this, but when the two met again at an inn, the Rummer and Horseshoe in Drury Lane, the man shouted him food and drink and renewed his pledge.

Passengers were not always as forgiving when Doyle robbed them. One family, whom Doyle had seen check into the Mermaid Inn in Windsor and planned to rob the next day, pulled out a **blunderbuss** when Doyle stopped their coach. Doyle, however, was a quick draw with his pistol, which he held to the man's nose and threatened to blow his head off if he continued to resist. Doyle took the **blunderbuss** first and then money, watches and other jewellery. The robbery also included a pocketbook full of money, with which the man had been going to pay his servants' wages.

Soon Doyle was back in London seeking entertainment. He found something to his taste at the Phoenix gambling house in the Haymarket. He took a short break during the evening to pawn some of the goods he'd stolen so that he could continue gambling and try to to win back what he'd lost, and add to it what he could. Luck was with him and he finally left before dawn with an extra £40 or so in his pocket.

Doyle's next port of call was Kent. He stabled his horse while he wandered around admiring the sights on foot. When doing this, he came across a gentleman, Sir Gregory Page, and lightened his pockets of 70 guineas, plus the usual rings and watches.

Back in London, Doyle took a six-month break from highway robbery and lived a relatively honest and quiet life for that time. He exercised his horse daily on the roads around Hampstead, Richmond and Hackney. This may have been purely for the horse's benefit and for his own enjoyment, but in so doing he also familiarised himself with all the main roads in that area. The knowledge stood him in good stead when he had to return to work because his funds needed replenishing.

The first victim in Doyle's new season of robbery was a Jewish gentleman carrying £75 plus bits and pieces. The next robbery was performed on a couple of Quakers that Doyle had targeted and followed from the Pack Horse Inn at Turnham Green. These two handed over £100, but he gave them back 1 guinea when they begged for some means to get to their destination. Doyle later saw in the papers that they'd been on their way to High Wycombe Market in Buckinghamshire to purchase wheat.

When he had put together a tidy sum, John Doyle returned to Ireland. He fell in love and wooed and won the woman, who agreed to be his wife. However, if he had thought that he'd be able to retire in comfort in his native land he certainly had to think again when he got married. Doyle's wife liked luxury and entertainment and these were expensive. It wasn't long before he had to go back on the road. This time he didn't go alone, but set up with a man who was known only by the initials N.B. They proved a formidable pair of highwaymen.

Doyle's success was also his downfall and he grew complacent in his robberies. He was arrested and taken to prison, but after much hard work and discomfort, he smashed off his leg irons and escaped. He fled to Waterford and arranged for his wife and his colleague to meet him there where they would all take passage to Bristol.

Unfortunately, the ship had to turn about and pull in at Cork because of bad weather and the three disembarked, fearful of being caught by the law if they stayed aboard. This strategy worked well and, on finding out the politics of the landlord of the inn in which they were staying, they claimed to be recruited men, fighting for the Pretender. This gave them not only an added respect from him, but also his loyalty and secrecy. The three had no intention of staying in Ireland and Doyle's wife was sent out to try to procure them passage to England. Unbeknownst to them, a thief-taker called Hawkins had followed them and recognised the woman as she went aboard a ship. Hawkins had Doyle's wife taken and questioned over her husband's whereabouts. The woman vehemently denied that Doyle was her husband and her lie was so convincing that the men who were to take her from the boat to the shore to gaol instead helped her disguise herself in some of their own clothes. In this manner, she was able to escape Hawkins and warn her husband about their imminent danger.

The trio then hired three horses and left Cork. In Limerick, Doyle swapped his hired hack for a decent horse and attempted to earn some money through hold-ups on the road. The pickings were very slim, however, and while he was engaged in seeking an income, his wife was arrested, tried and sentenced to transportation to America.

Distraught at her disappearance, Doyle bought a passage to Virginia as soon as he could and was able to track her down fairly quickly. He purchased her from William Dalton for £15 and the couple went to New York where the wife and her shame wouldn't be known. In the city, Doyle did meet up with some former acquaintances and enjoyed their society for a while. It was here that he heard of another man who had the same name. Thinking he might be related, he looked the man up and found that it was his uncle. They enjoyed each other's company for some time, but things turned sour when Doyle beat the servants, particularly those who were of an indigenous background. Doyle left his uncle's estate under a cloud and without money.

It may have been remorse that then persuaded Doyle to attempt to make an honest living working at his first trade, as a soap-boiler and tallow-chandler. The plan was that both he and his wife would work hard and save as much as they could and then return to England. They eventually managed to put together £200 and booked their passage home. Doyle sent his wife onto Ireland and said he would send for her when he had things settled for her in England. He swore to her that he had no intention of going back to his old ways of highway robbery. However, he obviously thought that what she didn't know wouldn't hurt her, because that was what he did as soon as he could. He joined up with a fearless companion and terrorised the roads around London, particularly the Hounslow and Hampstead areas. They become so notorious that the newspapers of the day wrote of their exploits and gave out detailed descriptions of what they both looked like. This invited too much danger of being reported to the law and they took off to Essex and then to Hertfordshire, robbing all the way.

On this journey, Doyle had a tip-off that a man was travelling the road with a purse of money tied under his arm and clothing. When the robbers approached him, they told him to strip, found the purse and took it. Later, when asked about the robbery and why he hadn't hurt the man, Doyle replied that it was the victim's business to try to keep his money safe, just as it was Doyle's to find it and take it.

Doyle was a man who believed in studying his victims before he robbed them. He wanted to know how much money they had on them and what their intended movements were. For example, Doyle and his partner once spent all day at a fair observing which people did the most trade and took the most money. These were then targeted as the next day's victims. Financially stable once again, Doyle made for Ireland to see his wife and their relatives. He shared out his money with the neediest of them and spent a lot of it on gambling; he loved horse racing. It wasn't long before his funds were depleted once again and he had to take to the road, following the familiar pattern of his life. Doyle then did another stint in England, this time teaming up with a villain called Benjamin Wileman. They undertook several robberies together, but were finally caught and sent to Newgate prison. The two supposed friends decided to give evidence against each other in an attempt to save their own necks. The outcome for Doyle was transportation along with his wife, where they both worked in the plantations of Virginia until he could secure their release. As soon as they had earned the money they went back to England. Yet almost as soon as they set foot on land, Doyle's wife was arrested for returning before she'd finished her sentence. Although she pleaded guilty to the charge, she obtained a pardon and was released.

In the meantime, Doyle was busy refilling the coffers by his usual methods. In Hungerford, while he was studying potential victims, an old acquaintance approached him and confessed that he was carrying a sum of money in the hope of deflecting an attack. He offered his address in London and promised him £1,000 in a month's time. Doyle agreed and he and his partner were all set to move their operation to another part of the country. Their plans, however, had to be changed at the last minute and they ended up in the same inn as the man with whom they had struck the deal. They drank a bottle of wine together and then mutually ignored each other for the rest of the evening.

Soon after, Doyle and his companion left for London. Their first port of call was the residence of the man they had promised not to rob and who had pledged them £1,000. It turned out that this man had been a highwayman himself at one time, but had given it all up to become a butcher and then a seller of cattle. They met, drank wine together and the £1,000 was handed over, plus the ex-highwayman offered tips as to who might be worth robbing.

Acting on the information given, Doyle and his companion stopped a chapman and took £250 from him. The man begged for some money to get home and the robbers handed 2 guineas back to him.

On returning to London, they revisited the cattle salesman-cum-ex-highwayman and gave him 50 guineas in return for his tip-off a few days before. The three men then began to plot out future deals. The salesman would tell the robbers which people had just received money from him and these would then be the targets for Doyle and co. Afterwards, Doyle would pay a commission to the salesman for his information.

While Doyle was a rogue, he was not as bad as some and seldom, if ever, resorted to violence. In fact, he often left the victim with some money to see them home. He also only robbed in the daytime, which meant that the county had to recompense the money and goods lost through highway robbery if the victim insisted on suing them, as it was the county's duty to keep the roads safe to travel.

After a season of slim pickings, Doyle spent some time living frugally and keeping out of public sight. During one of his forays out of his lodgings, however, he left his pistols behind and was subsequently arrested as he came out of an inn in Drury Lane. He did put up a fight, but it was a futile attempt without firearms and he was overpowered and taken to Newgate prison.

Doyle was hoping to avoid the death sentence and when it was handed down he confessed to being a Catholic not a

Protestant. He also confessed to having been a highway robber, but emphasised the fact he had never used violence on his victims. He also declared the love he had for his wife. At the point of execution, Doyle told the crowd that he'd left behind him his memoirs and that everything he had done was recounted, omitting nothing.

He was hanged on 30 June 1730. Doyle's wife arranged an elaborate funeral for him.

JAMES DRUMMOND

Born *c*. 1689 • Died 1729

James Drummond was the younger brother, by about ten years, of the highwayman Robert Drummond, whose history follows this one. James Drummond was left in the care of his paternal grandmother in London from the age of 3, when his sailor father died. We are not told where his brother Robert was at the time; quite possibly, he was already apprenticed out.

Instead of taking up an apprenticeship himself, James Drummond went to sea and became a highly capable navigator. For a long time he worked aboard man-of-war ships, travelling to Sweden and the Mediterranean and seeing action in both places.

Eventually, he retired from the navy and set up his own business dealing in china and other small goods. This involved a fair amount of travelling on land and could have given him ample opportunity to work as a highwayman, but he apparently didn't give in to the temptation until the beginning of 1729, after a drinking session with his brother Robert.

Robert was by now a seasoned highwayman and, on 19 October 1729, he took his brother to an inn and they both got quite drunk. It was in this state that Robert prevailed upon his younger brother to give highway robbery a go. Their first victim was Mr William Isgrig. Drummond mounted behind his brother and they set off. Two on a horse was too cumbersome, and Robert suggested that James should dismount and commit the robbery on foot while he covered him with his pistol from the horse. They took 16 guineas, 7 half-guineas, 3 **broad pieces**, 1 **moidore** and 20*s*, plus the man's watch: not a bad haul for a first-time robbery. They immediately set upon the next traveller who came by, a Mr Wakeling, from whom they took a few shillings and a silver watch. This victim, however, was not going to let them get away with the theft and pulled out his sword to defend himself and his property. When he realised that one of his attackers was on foot he chased him until he caught him and wrestled him to the ground. Robert had fired a couple of warning shots and then ridden off into the night to avoid capture.

James Drummond was arrested, tried for both robberies and was sentenced to death. His first thoughts were for the foolishness of his actions and the fact that he'd be abandoning his wife with five young children to look after (probably even more poignant to him as he had been orphaned so young himself). He was ashamed at having blemished his character as an honest, hardworking man and was conscious of the way it would taint his family.

A very repentant man, James Drummond was hanged for his one night of highway robbery on 22 December 1729.

ROBERT DRUMMOND
(ALIAS GODFREY; ALIAS BELL)

Born *c.* 1679 • Died 1730

Robert Drummond was at least 13 years old when his father died. His little brother James was left in the care of their grandmother, but nothing is recorded of where Robert went. As a young adult, he lived in Sunderland and sold hardware. He had a very good reputation amongst the townsfolk, who thought he was an upstanding citizen. However, he had already been practising highway robbery for some time. When he finally abandoned the disguise of an honest shop-keeper for that of a robber, Drummond was soon caught, tried and transported to the colonies.

As with many felons, the call of home was too much and he managed to get passage back to England before his seven years were up. As soon as he was on shore, he took up his old occupation.

By all accounts, Robert Drummond was no gentleman rogue but a violent and merciless villain. He had no qualms about abusing his victims either, whether they put up a resistance or gave in quietly.

Ferdinando Shrimpton and his cousin William were two of Robert Drummond's main accomplices. They supposedly committed a spate of highway robberies for which another two men, both known highwaymen, were convicted and executed: Henry Knowland and Thomas Westwood.

When he was finally caught, Drummond gave evidence against his friends, but was sentenced to hang for aiding, abetting and assisting in the murder of Simon Prebent, coachman to a Mr Tyson, during a robbery on Mr Tyson (Ferdinando was accused of the actual murder), attacking and robbing Robert Furnel on the highway and committing a similar offence against Jonathon Cockhoofs on the highway, plus taking his horse and several roasting pigs. Both Drummond and Shrimpton refused to confess to the crimes that Knowland and Westwood were hanged for, asking why should they confess to every highway robbery committed in England. Drummond showed no remorse for any of the crimes for which he was convicted, or any sorrow over having been the cause of his brother's death.

The ordinary of Newgate says that while Ferdinando Shrimpton, Drummond's partner in crime, showed ample signs of remorse, Drummond showed almost none and only attended chapel once or twice. After that, he claimed that he was ill but, the ordinary says, it was probably so he could plan his escape. He was going to put his plan into action on the night of 15 March 1729 but was caught in the act. After this, he was put in double irons and moved to a more secure cell. Drummond still refused to attend chapel, but stayed in bed instead.

Robert Drummond was hanged at Tyburn along with Ferdinando Shrimpton on 17 February 1730.

ANTHONY DRURY

Born *c*. 1698 • Died 1726

Not much is known of Anthony Drury's early life. He was born into a middle-class family in Norfolk, where he was educated, and made a name for himself as a doctor of smoking chimneys in Oxford. While in this trade, he married a rich widow from the area, which set him up to be a gentleman of leisure. Rumour has it that Drury was very much one for the ladies and, despite having a wife, was very keen to seek out the company of women to whom he was not married. Apparently, his wife was rather long suffering on this account.

Why he took to highway robbery can only be speculated upon, but on 25 September 1726 he ambushed the Bicester coach from London and took from its occupants 15 **moidores**, 200 guineas, 80 half-guineas, plus assorted jewellery. He also stopped, assaulted and robbed Sarah King as she travelled, although she only had 2*s* and sixpence on her. Despite his love of women, this did not stop him robbing them, and he assaulted another one not long after Sarah. This time it was a Mary Page who also only carried a couple of shillings with her.

Drury was caught and indicted for these offences and, while he languished in gaol, he begged his wife to come and see him. Yet his words fell on deaf ears, even when he asked a third party to beseech her on his behalf. The friend wrote back to Drury and told him that his wife was ill and incapacitated. Her money was gone and she lived alone in poverty. This may or may not have been true. Drury tried one last time to get her to visit him by concocting a story about some gold plate that he had pawned that would be lost on his death. He bid his friend tell his wife this. The friend answered Drury with a short note saying that Mrs Drury would be very pleased if somebody in town could release the plate and bring it to her.

She would even give them a reward, but there was no way that she was going to see her husband face to face.

Drury refused to plead guilty to any of the crimes with which he was charged. The robbery of the Bicester wagon was, he said, the idea of the wagoner himself, who happened to be the husband of Mary King, the woman he was supposed to have assaulted. Drury claimed that he and King hatched a plot to rob the wagon and then split the takings. Drury was then to rob King's wife in attempt to throw anyone off the scent.

Although Drury remained adamant that the wagoner was involved in the Bicester robbery, it had no effect on his own sentence and was not heeded by the authorities. Drury, therefore, prepared himself for his coming execution.

While in Newgate prison, Drury lived in relatively comfortable surroundings in a room of his own. He received several visits from a young woman of whom nothing is known except that he called her as witness to having overheard some of the conversations between himself and King.

Through his persistent attempts to have someone take his version of events seriously, Drury managed to get a number of influential people to put forward a petition for his release, but it was futile. He still held hopes of a pardon as late as the night before his execution when another woman visited him and asked for the details of the case. But it wasn't to be. Drury was taken to Tyburn gallows the following day. At his public speech he repeated his story about the wagoner and said that he forgave him and that he also forgave his wife for having abandoned him in his hour of need.

Drury was hanged on 3 November 1726.

WILLIAM DUCE

Born *c*. 1698 • Died 1723

Nothing is known of William Duce's early life except that he was born in Wolverhampton. The first we hear of him is his arrest for debt and his incarceration in Newgate. He resided there for well over a year. This stint in prison, making acquaintance with all sorts of undesirable sorts, was, it is said, the cause of Duce's descent into highway robbery.

Duce became part of highwayman John Dyer's gang, which included Butler and Rice, among others. Duce's first victim was a well-armed man walking across Chelsea Fields. Duce and another gang member, after some deliberation as to whether the man should be approached or not, came up on either side of him and grabbed his arms so that he could not wield his sword or his walking stick. When the man was tied up behind a hedge, the two took the contents of his pocket, which only amounted to 4 guineas.

The next victim was a woman out strolling. They took what she had and then jumped over a nearby wall without harming her. It was going well, but Duce found Dyer a hard man to work for. Dyer was a bully and would often threaten Duce with violence if he didn't perform certain robberies. Often those in which he was involved were hardly worth the risk for the meagre takings, being a guinea or two or a watch.

The gang eventually moved its operations to the countryside around Hampshire. The robberies they committed there were accompanied by extreme violence. One victim, Mr Bunch, was shot in the cheek by Duce after he'd been robbed and stripped of his clothes. The bullet fell from the wound when the man turned his face to the ground. Butler then began shooting at him although he begged for his life. By a miracle, Mr Bunch was able to stagger off while Butler was recharging his pistol. He made it to the nearest village and raised the alarm.

Consequently, the members of the gang were caught. Some were sent to Winchester, but Butler and Duce were sent straight to Newgate. Once in prison, Duce became a different man, resigning himself to death and giving evidence against the gang leader, Dyer. Duce also wrote a letter to Dyer, urging him to repent for his crimes and to beg God for forgiveness. Duce then finished by offering his own forgiveness for the crimes that Dyer had tempted him to do, accepting his own guilt as being his sole responsibility.

William Duce was hanged at Tyburn on 5 August 1723.

CLAUDE DUVAL

Born 1643 • Died 1670

Claude Duval is the epitome of the gentlemanly highwayman. Dashing, brave and courteous; to be robbed by Claude Duval was to be paid the highest compliment. In fiction perhaps, but what of the reality? Is it possible to sort the truth from the tales or has Duval's name become like that of Katherine Ferrers and Dick Turpin, so covered in fabulous detail, so elaborated over the years that there is hardly any of the original left?

Duval is the anglicised form of the French *du Val*. There are numerous variations on the spelling. Duval was a Frenchman by birth (Normandy, to be exact). His father was a miller and his mother was the daughter of a tailor (which may explain the highwayman's penchant for fashionable clothes). They were devout Catholics and brought their son up to be the same.

The young Duval was prepared for employment as a footman. He may have worked in this capacity for a short time, but eventually changed over to the stables and looked after and then rode post horses, embracing his passion for riding. This employment led him to meet a group of English gentlemen

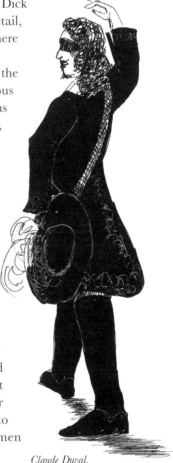

Claude Duval.

119

who took him under their wing and got him a job running errands at the St Esprit: a popular place of entertainment, drink and prostitution.

When Charles II returned to the English throne in 1660, the Royalists, with whom Duval felt himself indebted, were able to go home too and they took the young man with them to be their footman. England was giddy with joy at the return of their king and it became a time of excess. Duval was only too willing to join in the general rejoicing by indulging in gambling, drinking and women: all things that cost more money than a humble footman earned. Consequently, Duval turned to robbing the highway to support his addictions.

Highway robbery was Duval's forte. He became so notorious in such a short time that his name topped the list of wanted men. He supposedly didn't resort to violence during his holdups and was especially courteous, gallant even, to the young ladies. It was because of this that he earned an early reputation as something of a gentleman thief. This is illustrated in the story of Duval stopping a coach in which a young lady was playing her flageolet. The highwayman just happened to have his own instrument in his coat pocket and pulled it out to join her in a duet. When the music finished, instead of getting straight to the business and demanding the traveller's money, Duval opened the coach door and requested a dance with the lady. The woman's husband said that he wouldn't dare to deny the robber anything and watched as the two danced in the dirt of the highway.

When they'd finished, Duval saw the lady back into the coach and then politely told the gentleman within that he had forgotten to pay for the music. Without hesitation, the traveller pulled a bag from under his seat containing £100 and handed it over, saying that he never forgot anything. Duval took the money and answered that the generous payment made voluntarily would save the man the remaining £300 hidden in the coach. He then bade them good day.

By contrast, there is a story in which Duval stopped a coach full of ladies, one with a young child who was sucking on a silver bottle. Duval robbed them of every little thing of value, including the child's bottle. He is said to have behaved very rudely to the women and only gave the child's bottle back when his companions urged him to do so. Perhaps Duval's chivalry did not extend to wailing children.

Although Duval didn't have a reputation for using violence on his victims, he wasn't above tying them up and abandoning them in the woods, as he did to one poor huntsman before relieving him of his valuables.

When England grew too hot to hold him any longer, Claude Duval returned to France and lived the high life in Paris where he devised a cunning plan to dupe a greedy priest, confessor, to the king. Duval, disguised as a scholar, approached the priest and told him he was an alchemist and could turn base metal into gold. The priest set Duval up in a laboratory and watched eagerly as the 'alchemist' put metal into a crucible and then stirred it with a rod. As the metal heated, gold appeared in the bottom of the crucible. Duval had filled the hollow rod with slivers of gold and the heat caused them to melt and run out the rod.

The amazing result of the alchemical process gave the priest confidence in Duval and he showed him his treasure hoard. Duval slipped into the priest's house one afternoon, bound and gagged the sleeping priest, took his keys, stole as much gold and jewels as he could carry, and fled back to England.

Duval was a skilful gambler and often supplemented his robbery earnings with winnings from cards, and vice versa. He is also supposed to have been a terrible ladies' man, full of flattery and flirting. His vices, however, were eventually his downfall and he was finally apprehended while drunk at an inn called the Hole-In-The-Wall in Chandos Street. He was taken straight to Newgate and hanged on 21 January 1670.

After his death, his body was cut down and taken to the Tangier tavern in St Giles to be laid out for a night. While his body was there, a note was found in one of his pockets. It was a flowery love letter to all the beautiful women of England, thanking them all for receiving someone born as lowly as he was; he loved them all.

Claude Duval was buried under the central aisle of St Paul's Church, Covent Garden and his epitaph reads as follows:

Here lies Du Vall: Reder, if male thou art,
Look to thy purse; if female, to thy heart.
Much havoc has he made of both; for all
Men he made to stand, and women he made to fall.
The second Conqueror of the Norman race,
Knights to his arm did yield, and ladies to his face.
Old Tyburn's glory; England's illustrious Thief,
Du Vall, the ladies' joy; Du Vall, the ladies' grief.

JOHN DYKES

Born *c*. 1698 • Died 1721

John Dykes came from a relatively comfortable background. According to the records he was the eldest son of rather indulgent parents. When it came time to consider his future employment he couldn't think of anything he really wanted to do and blankly refused to sign up as an apprentice. He had also developed a gambling addiction very young and whatever money he could obtain went on the gaming tables in town. When he was skint he'd play **chucks** and **span-farthing** in the streets with whoever was hanging around. If he won enough he'd go back to the tables. Eventually, he added pickpocketing to his activities as a way to fund his addiction. Yet Dykes was not such an adept thief that he didn't get caught sometimes. In fact, he was often in and out of Bridewell. His family would pay to get him out and he would promise to reform. A popular punishment that was used at the time was a ducking in the horse pond, and Dykes received a fair few of these.

During one of his stays in Bridewell, Dykes met with Jeddediah West and the two decided that they would go into partnership. West then wrote to his brother from the prison claiming his innocence of his crime and asked him for help in getting out. Copying West's example, Dykes tried the same trick on his parents. Both young men found gullible targets in their relatives and were soon released from gaol.

After their liberation, Dykes and West frequently met up at the gambling tables. For three weeks after their release, they were successful and this success spurred them on to larger and higher stakes at the tables. However, it also took no more than three weeks for them to lose all the money they had won. Neither of them could face returning to the families that they had made promises to about turning over new leaves and quitting gambling, and so they had to think up another way to refill the coffers.

West dressed himself as a sailor and had his hair cut short to complete the illusion that he had signed up on board a ship. His brother asked him what was going on and West replied that he had met some coiners in Bridewell who had decided to use him as a method of getting themselves off their charges by turning evidence against him. West was then obliged to flee the country or risk being sent down for theft and possibly executed. He was, therefore, throwing himself on his brother's charity one last time.

West's brother fell for the story, handed him 10 guineas immediately with the promise of a £100 more in Dieppe (where West was supposed to be sailing) from the bank, withdrawn in the brother's name. Of course, there was no such plot against West and he had no intention of sailing to Dieppe. Instead, he took a coach to the place that he had agreed to meet Dykes. The two then went off together in great glee at their cleverness. West's trick, however, was soon discovered by his family and they disowned him. West was then arrested and charged with owing his tailor £12.

Dykes, now on his own, would go robbing on the highway to get money for gambling. His last robbery was committed on the road between Mile End and Bow in Stepney. His victim was Charles Wright. Dykes held a pistol to the man's chest and threatened to pull the trigger if he didn't hand over his valuables. The haul only amounted to a penknife, a wax seal and 5s 8d.

Two days later, Dykes was arrested for this robbery and taken to Newgate. The trial led to a sentence of hanging. After the sentence was pronounced, Dykes confessed to all the other crimes of which he was guilty. He was hanged at Tyburn on 23 October 1721.

West made yet another appeal to his brother for financial help and was released again after Dykes's death.

JOHN DYER

Born *c*. 1698 • Died 1729

John Dyer was a highwayman who was the antithesis of a gentleman. Not only did he commit highway robbery and other kinds of theft, but also rape. He had a tendency to stay with a woman until she got pregnant and then he would abandon her.

He was born in Salisbury and, when old enough, apprenticed to a shoemaker. He began his thieving while still a youth and under apprenticeship. One of his first robberies was the money box from a chandler's shop. After the success of this, he would often commit thefts while on errands for his master to a shop in the village. Dyer broke into the place when he found nobody there, took what little cash there was and then helped himself to dried fruit. When the break-in was discovered, the owners immediately suspected Dyer and had him searched. He had already hidden the money and claimed that he'd bought the dried fruit from the market. It was impossible to prove his guilt and he walked free.

The next major incident involved £5 that his master had given him to buy leather. Dyer, with the help of a friend, pretended that he'd been robbed on his way to purchase the leather. He called his friend as a witness to the supposed robbery. The master believed the tale and Dyer continued his criminal ways, steadily growing worse with them.

Another time, he was sent to pick up money owed by customers. Dyer used it on a prostitute in Salisbury. In order to pay it back, he went to the market to see what he could pilfer. Once there, he saw a young woman being given some money and he set her as his target for robbery. He followed her as she left town and, when no one was around, he grabbed her, dragged her into the wood, raped her and left her tied to a tree before running off with her money.

After his apprenticeship was over, Dyer made his home in Hampshire and set up as a journeyman shoemaker. He met a girl in the village and moved in with her. When she got pregnant, Dyer plotted with her to rob her mother and flee to Bristol. The theft was a success, but they got through the money quickly and ended up going their separate ways; she and the baby went back to her mother and Dyer went off to visit his own mother in Salisbury. Dyer didn't go to see her out of any filial duty, but in order to sponge from her and then rob her outright before taking off to Bristol again. The £50 he took from her mostly ended up on the gaming tables. From Bristol he made his way to Wiltshire and found a widow who was happy to take him in. The pair of them racked up credit to the value of £30. Instead of trying to pay up, however, the two of them did a moonlight flit.

Dyer then set up in business with a collier, but the partnership didn't last. The collier went broke and left Dyer short by £30. Dyer went to Hereford and actually set himself up in honest work. What became of the widow he had lived with is not said.

Dyer's determination to live a hardworking, honest life didn't last beyond him meeting a **higler** who suggested that they go together to a place to buy poultry. Dyer robbed his companion of the money with which he was going to buy the birds, plus his horse.

Dyer then rode to Marlborough, a distance of 40 miles. In Wiltshire, his next stop, he was caught stealing a silver mug. He would probably have been found guilty and sentenced to hang for that crime, but he managed to escape.

From breaking out of gaol, Dyer went and hid at his aunt's house until his uncle-in-law started making noises about what was to be done about him and how they'd all get into trouble if he was found hidden in their house. Dyer took the hint and went to stay with his sister instead. It was here that he renewed an old friendship with someone he could easily influence to go to town with him to seek amusement: gambling. To fund this expedition Dyer got the friend to steal £50 from his mother. When the theft was noticed there was an outcry about it and the son of the victim and his friend were accused outright. On Dyer's urging, the young man denied it, but it was not believed and the two men were taken before a local Justice of the Peace. He sent them to Bridewell to undergo a period of hard labour.

Dyer had already managed an escape from one gaol; his second was no harder. It is thought that Dyer and his companion got out of Bridewell by jumping down into the cess pool. It was after this second escape from prison that Dyer took up highway robbery. He was an expert horse thief, so never found himself without a suitable mount.

He was the kind of highwayman who didn't discriminate between robbing rich and poor, male and female, and even stole the clothes of a maid-servant. It was when he sold the clothes in Winchester that he made friends with a lace dealer who was on his way to the Amesbury Fair in Wiltshire. They travelled along together and even stayed at the same inn, The Chopping Knife. The lace dealer left his new friend at the inn while he went to establish a spot for his stall at the upcoming fair. While he was away, Dyer stole the man's box of lace and rode off with it.

The next victim was a pedlar selling handkerchiefs and similar small goods. Dyer stopped him as if he were interested in purchasing something, but instead demanded he be given what he wanted from the man. The pedlar tried to defend himself and his goods, but Dyer pulled out his pistol and threatened him with it, then tied the poor fellow up with his own linen and took as much as he could carry of the pedlar's stock, which included a quantity of human hair. To be fair, Dyer untied the man at the end of his looting session and told him to get back to what was left of his wares. The human hair was sold to a wig maker for £80.

Yet another of Dyer's robberies was made against an old shepherd on his way back from market. When Dyer told him to hand over his money the old man tried to fight him off with his crook. Although he put up a good fight, the shepherd lost in the end and Dyer took £70 of his market earnings.

The spate of robberies meant that Dyer was in possession of reasonable funds and was able to go to Dorchester to spend it. Unsurprisingly, he got through the money quickly and was soon on the road again, but this time he had a new companion, a butcher whose business had gone bust. The butcher, however, had bigger plans than to rob unwary travellers; he thought he'd go for Dyer as well, a plan that could so easily have got him killed. Dyer overlooked the little misdemeanour and made the butcher promise not to do anything like it again.

The pair went on to rob a cheese maker whom they had observed making over £80 at a fair. They stopped him outside the town and were furious to find that the man had used a lot of the funds to pay his debts. They whipped him and told him to never go paying bills while there were highwaymen ready to take care of it for him.

Another time they robbed a hop merchant. When they couldn't find any money on him they threatened to kill the man, but then his wife called out and told them that he had it hidden in his boots. Dyer and his partner thanked the woman as they rode off with her husband's income in their pockets.

After all their hard work it was time for some respite and as each had a mistress in Sherbourne that was the town they headed for. Predictably, the holiday ended when the money was spent and they had to go back to work, taking a rich grazier for £90. Not long after this, the butcher got sick and the pair was forced to take another break in Ringwood. The butcher's illness ate up a lot of the money they had taken from the grazier, but they were soon up and robbing again, doing a regular job on the road from Bath to London. One coachman fired his **blunderbuss** at them, missed and was whipped for having had the audacity to try to stop them.

In Hungerford, Dyer found a suitable wife, the widow of a butcher, for his butcher friend. Unfortunately, Dyer and the butcher were discovered to be highwaymen and the wedding was cancelled. It also meant that they had to flee the town.

Their last robbery together was of a tallow chandler. They felt that they should split up for safety's sake after this. The butcher returned to Devonshire and Dyer went to see his sister in Salisbury again before he set off for London.

Whatever got into Dyer cannot be guessed, but as soon as he got to London he settled down to the shoemaking trade and, for a whole year, existed on these earnings only. It would be too much to believe that he was totally reformed, and, whatever the reason, it couldn't last. He found a lady friend who was very keen on money and luxuries that she couldn't afford, so it was back on the highway to pay for the bail to keep her out of debtors' prison.

Not only was Dyer's mistress a spendthrift, she was also married and one morning the pair was surprised by her husband coming home from sea. His reaction was to see Dyer clapped in prison. Dyer had no trouble getting bail, however, and got his own back on the man by having him arrested for the debt of feeding and lodging his wife for nine months. The husband finally paid Dyer the £10 demanded of him and got out of the compter.

It was with a new resolution of honesty that Dyer, having ditched his extravagant mistress, found a respectable woman to marry and settled down to a cobbler's stall in Leather Lane. But the call of the open road proved stronger than Dyer's love and commitment to his new wife, and it was not long before he had found a highway partner (a local man having financial difficulties) with whom to resume his former occupation. They did a number of hold-ups in the Lincoln's Fields area until too many watchmen had been put on guard to grab them.

From this partnership, Dyer went on to bigger things and joined a gang who robbed at Blackheath. Dyer, from whose memoirs all these recounts are taken, says little of his time with the gang. This is probably because when they all got arrested he turned evidence against them, for which they were hanged and he was saved. This, we infer from its absence in his own records, is because he felt some shame at this act of betrayal. He did, however, spend seven years in Newgate for his part in the robberies with which they were all charged.

When he was eventually let out, along with a man called Abraham Dumbleton, the recorder at Newgate issued them with a stern warning that if either were caught at their old business they would be hanged. He suggested that they apply for a voluntary transportation to one of the colonies to prevent them falling into their old ways. Both prisoners declined, but promised they'd be law-abiding citizens this time. Yet neither had any intention of keeping their promise and they were soon out together terrifying travellers around London.

Their ultimate downfall came a relatively short time after their release from Newgate. They robbed a Mr Bradley in Hatton Garden, taking his hat and wig and pushing him over then bashing him up. As the watch came running to the man's defence the two robbers fired their pistols and got away. A couple of nights after this outrageous attack, Dyer and Dumbleton made their very last robbery, breaking into a draper's shop and stealing linen. How and when they were arrested we don't know, but they were both found guilty and sentenced, as they had been warned, to death by hanging.

While waiting for his sentence to be carried out, Dyer wrote down all the exploits that he felt he could own up to without shame. In fact, he dwelt on the less aggressive and the more humorous ones. The memoir was published the day before his death to a public with an insatiable hunger for all the details of crime and its subsequent punishment. He at least pretended to be sorry for all the crimes he had committed, although the tone of his memoir suggests otherwise. He was hanged on 21 November 1729.

JOHN EVERETT

Born *c.* 1686 • Died 1729/30

John Everett was born in Polson, Hertfordshire. He was in the process of training to be a salesman when he decided to sign-up and go to fight in Flanders. A military career seemed to roll out before him; he did so well that he was made a sergeant in General How's regiment. When peace descended between nations, however, Everett's position became superfluous and he returned home to unemployment.

For seven years, Everett worked successfully for a bailiff's office. Unfortunately, it was at this time that he also made friends with a man who had criminal connections. The details of what happened are not recorded but somehow, through his acquaintance with the criminal, Everett found he was in danger of going to prison. One of his options, in order to avoid a sentence, was to re-enlist in the army. He thus joined the Foot Guards under the Earl of Albermarle, but this did not prove to be the shelter he'd hoped. Another of his old acquaintances, a man by the name of Richard 'Dick' Bird whom he had met through his previous criminal connections, caught up with him and persuaded him to go robbing with him on the highways.

Middlesex, Essex, Surrey and Kent were their particular favourite courses, from which they could hold-up the Dartford coach. Their regular haul consisted of money, watches and various bits of jewellery. It wasn't a bad income, but they both spent it at a faster rate than they made it.

Everett was also no stranger to the code of courtesy associated with highwaymen. For example, when the duo robbed the Woodford stagecoach, the only person travelling on it was a gentleman who was very upset at handing over his watch. Everett and Bird made a deal with him that if he met them at a prearranged destination they would give him his watch back. Amazingly, this type of arrangement was used quite a lot between highway robbers and their victims, with both parties sticking to their side of the bargain.

Another robbery committed on Hounslow Heath resulted in a similar deal being struck between the highwaymen and two army officers from whom they had stolen two watches. The agreement made between the two pairs of men led to the items being left at Young Man's Coffee House, Charing Cross. It cost the officers 20 guineas each to retrieve their own property back.

Compared to some, John Everett and Dick Bird were not such a bad pair of highwaymen. They seldom, if ever, resorted to violence and they were happy to offer back items at an agreed price. They also didn't take everything a victim had, such as the clothes they wore, their horses or even their dignity.

During Everett's confinement in prison, he told the ordinary that he hated violence and would never fire a pistol at another person. He was recorded saying, 'I ever abhorred barbarity, or the more heinous sin of murder.' Indeed, according to the thief's own version of some of their crimes, it would seem that the attraction of robbery was not mere monetary gain, but the interaction between themselves and the men and women they held up. One such entertaining encounter occurred when Everett fancied a **bob wig** that sat atop the head of a Quaker seated in a coach with a number of other passengers. Everett pulled it off the man's head and swapped it with his own second-hand **tie wig** (which he had bought, not stolen). The **tie wig** made the man look like a comical devil and the rest of the coach party burst out laughing. The robbery ended with all parties going their separate ways without any hard feelings (except perhaps from the Quaker). The highwaymen even gave the coachman 1s to drink their health.

Everett was arrested soon after this and detained in New Prison for three years. He was subsequently let out for good behaviour and given the post of turnkey at the gaol. It looked as though his life had taken a new turn and soon he was able to leave his position as turnkey and take on the licence at the Red Lion Inn in Turnmill Street. He returned as turnkey for a while longer at the request of the next incumbent, but in the end he was forced to leave because the gaol keeper wanted the position for his own brother.

From then on, Everett spent time running various ale houses and sitting in a debtors' prison, as he always lived beyond his means. During his last stint in the debtors' prison the brewer who supplied Everett's alehouse took back all his beer, so that when Everett was free again he had nothing to sell and no way to make an honest living. It was back to the highway.

Back on the road, he stuck to the old code of avoiding violence or even the semblance of it. On holding up a woman in a coach and her 6-year-old child, he put his pistol away out of sight, so that he didn't frighten them. All he took from the woman was some money, leaving her personal valuables untouched.

In the end, his neighbours reported him, suspecting that he was up to no good. Everett was arrested and taken to Newgate yet again. In a last attempt to have his sentence transmuted, he wrote a letter to one of his recent, female victims, expressing his great sorrow at having caused her distress and explaining that he was only trying to raise £50 so that he could set himself up in an alehouse. With this letter he hoped that the woman would take pity on him and petition for his release. His hope, though, was in vain.

John Everett was hanged in February of 1729 or 1730. His one-time companion, Dick Bird, had been arrested and hanged long before on the impeachment of Everett himself.

RICHARD FERGUSON

Birthdate Unknown • Died 1800

Richard Ferguson was born in Herefordshire. His father was a gentlemen's servant and travelled constantly with his master. It is suggested that this lack of paternal attention gave rise to the wild behaviour of the boy. At 15, Ferguson's father had him employed as a stable boy with the coachman of his master. It appeared to be work that suited the young man's temperament and he became adept at handling horses.

What appears to have been the trigger of his moral decline was his temporary promotion to **postilion**. He had enjoyed the new position so much that when he had to revert to his former job as stable boy he decided to look for a new employer. As luck would have it, he was taken on the same afternoon by a lady known to the master's family. She asked for Ferguson specifically, having admired him when he had been acting **postilion**.

He was happily employed in his new position with his new mistress and may well have stayed on the right side of the law, if he hadn't been caught in a compromising situation with one of the servant girls. The outraged mistress dismissed him at once. From then on, Ferguson's career declined. He went from situation to situation, always ending up out on his ear for drunkenness or laziness.

Even after this, he might have saved himself from the gallows; his father left him £57 in his will and, finding he no longer needed to earn his keep, he decided to become a gentleman. Unfortunately, he could not resist acting as if he were a man of true wealth and frittered away the money on clothes and the theatre. It was at Drury Lane that he fell for the charms of a young prostitute named Nancy who, taking him for someone of wealth, caught him hook, line and sinker.

In order to visit his love regularly, Ferguson secretly took on work as a **postilion** with an inn in Piccadilly. All his earnings went on Nancy and in this he was not alone. She had many lovers, several of whom were noted highwaymen. In fact, it was one of these lovers, a man called Abershaw, who once held up a coach with which Ferguson was riding as **postilion**. When Abershaw's mask slipped the two men recognised each other. Abershaw, worried that Ferguson might turn him in, arranged to meet him and offered him money in return for his continued silence. Ferguson, more than happy to take the money, rushed off to visit his lover, but he was turned away. She had discovered his true position and told him that she was otherwise engaged. It seems that Ferguson didn't see her again.

Returning to his home, Ferguson fell in with Abershaw's colleagues and he was invited to join their band. The part he played was not one of hands-on robber, but as a gatherer of information through his position at the inn. Ferguson was able to tell the gang who was driving where, with whom and what the possible haul would be. However, drunkenness once again led to him losing his employment at the inn and, without his insider knowledge, he could no longer perform his duties for the gang. He had to take to the road himself.

On the road, Ferguson's riding skills set him above the rest. In fact, during one of his hold-ups he was able to escape easily whereas his two companions were caught and later executed. His excellent riding skills were also something that he later became fond of boasting about and they earned him the nickname of Galloping Dick. Ferguson gained a reputation as a ladies' man, often engaging in amorous intrigue, particularly with married women who fell for the tales of his daring exploits. He enjoyed a lengthy career as a highway robber, but the law finally caught up with him. He was arrested for a robbery undertaken in Aylesbury, Bucks and was sentenced to hang.

Towards the end, he acknowledged his bad deeds and repented in the hope that God would pardon him his earthly sins. He was executed in 1800.

KATHERINE FERRERS

Born 1634 • Died 1660

This is the one that we have all been waiting to read about. The courageous, beautiful young woman whose exploits have become the stuff of legend. Unfortunately, much of what is said of Ferrers is little more than fiction. What we do know is that someone existed in Ferrers's time, meeting her description, who committed a large number of outrageous crimes, including highway robbery, burglary, arson, cattle theft and at least one murder. For the purposes of this book, we will treat the historical Katherine Ferrers as the perpetrator of the crimes with which she is charged in popular legend.

Ferrers grew up in the turbulent times of the English Civil War when highway robbery was rife. There were Cavaliers swearing oaths to rob only Roundheads, and Roundheads taking revenge on Cavalier highwaymen; ex-Parliamentarian soldiers eking out a livelihood by robbing on the roads and gangs of organised criminals causing strife everywhere. In Ferrers's part of the world, Hertfordshire, it is claimed that when she died in 1660 many of the crimes ceased.

Katherine Ferrers.

The Ferrers had an ancient family estate called Markyate Cell, in

Hertfordshire. Her father, Sir Knighton, lived alone with his own elderly parent, Sir George Ferrers, in the large house until he married a beautiful young heiress called Katherine Walters. Apparently, a boy was born to the couple, but he didn't live past infancy. A second child, Katherine, was born a couple of months after her father died. On the death of her grandfather, shortly after her birth, Ferrers became the heiress of the extensive Markyate Cell estate. Ferrers's mother returned to her own family home after the death of her husband and father-in-law to live within the comfort and support of the community she knew.

When young Ferrers was about 6 years old, her mother married Simon Fanshawe, a close neighbour of her late husband, who was a staunch Royalist and got heavily involved in the English Civil War. One account says that Fanshawe had to flee his own estate at Ware when it was invaded by Roundhead soldiers and that his wife and step-daughter took refuge with Lady Bethell at Hammerton in Huntingdonshire. Apart from this anomaly, most accounts agree that Katherine Fanshawe died only two years after her new marriage.

With a step-daughter coming up to marriageable age and with problems of his own, Simon Fanshawe had young Ferrers made a ward of the court by her step-uncle, Richard Fanshawe, and sent her to the previously mentioned Lady Bethell (or Bedell as she is also referred to).

Marriage in the seventeenth century was not about love or romance, but about the building of fortunes and the establishment of enormous estates. In short, it was a business proposition. Ferrers was to inherit her grandfather's estate of Markyate Cell, which adjoined land owned by her step-father. It is no surprise, therefore, that just before she turned 14 she was married off to Simon's nephew Thomas Fanshawe. One account suggests that Thomas was not Simon's nephew at all, but his own son, making Ferrers the bride of her own step-brother. Yet it must be remembered that Ferrers had been made over as a ward of court, so was no longer legally part of Simon's family and there would therefore have been nothing untoward in her marrying Thomas Fanshawe.

To be married so young was not unusual; the legal age of marriage at this time was 12. With life so hard and often short, this would not have seemed as inappropriate as it does to the modern reader. However, their marriage wasn't to last. The reason for this is up for speculation. Probably one of the main reasons would have been Thomas's part in the Civil War. Sixteen was not seen as too young to fight for one's cause, especially when it was for the king. Whatever the cause, Katherine Ferrers returned to her own estates at Markyate without kin.

At this point, there would have been no income as the Parliament under Cromwell had frozen or seized anything belonging to the Royalists. If Lady Ferrers then turned to highway robbery she would only have been following many of her contemporaries into the profession. Many displaced Royalists became highway robbers, not just to earn money to live, but also to seek revenge on their dead king. What was unusual in Ferrers's case was the fact that she was female.

As a highwaywoman, Ferrers earned a ruthless and savage reputation. She is said to have dressed in her three-cornered hat, men's breeches, cloak and mask and left her home at night by means of a secret passageway. Her hunting ground was Nomansland Common at Wheathampstead, which is not very close to Markyate Cell and the distance has caused problems of logistics in the tales of Ferrers's crimes. Another story has put forward the idea that she had a hideout in Gustard Wood, to the north of Wheathampstead, and it was from this base that she would ride forth. This proposition makes sense also if the Markyate Cell estates had been sold out of the family's hands.

Legend has it that she teamed up with a local farmer, Ralph Chaplin, in her nocturnal adventures on the highway.

She would meet him some distance away with the horses all ready. Ferrers's horse was black with white flashes on its fore-legs. The advantages of a black horse at night would be its almost invisibility, although the white flashes would be a bit of a giveaway.

The robberies that Ferrers and Chaplin committed were violent and often without mercy. They are even said to have murdered victims during the course of their hold-ups. One of Ferrers's methods of surprising an unsuspecting traveller was to wait in a tree overhanging the road and drop out in front of the coach, pistols drawn.

Ralph Chaplin died before Ferrers. Some accounts say that he was shot dead during an attempted robbery. Others say that he was captured on Finchley Common, 20 miles from Nomansland Common. From there he was tried, sentenced and hanged for highway robbery.

In her grief at Chaplin's death – so the legend goes – Ferrers exacted a terrifying revenge on the people of her area. She shot dead a constable on his own doorstep (this account is questionable though, since the formal constable role was not established for another century or more), slaughtered cattle and burned families in their homes as the slept.

Ferrers's ultimate fate is another mystery. The most popular story is that she held up a wagon of supplies headed for an inn near Gustard Wood. Ferrers shot the driver dead on the spot, but she didn't notice an armed passenger amongst the goods that the wagon was carrying and she was hit by a bullet. It didn't kill her straightaway and she managed to get home, but she died there soon afterwards. In one account, she got as far as the door to her secret passage at Markyate Cell.

Apparently, there really was a secret door with a passage or room behind it, which was not at all uncommon in those big old houses. The door was bricked over and not rediscov-ered until a fire broke out in the house in 1840 (Ferrers's ghost being blamed for the fire). The hidden oak door was broken down to find out what was behind it. Later, the hidden spring, still in working order, was discovered. The workmen who had broken through had hoped to find the hidden treasure that the highwaywoman was said to have stored away somewhere on her estate. The room to which the passage led, however, was empty.

A little rhyme arose about the treasure:

Near the cell there is a well
Near the well there is a tree
And under the tree the treasure be

The Wicked Lady.

Another, less dramatic version of Ferrers's death is that she died in childbirth. This was a very common way to die for women of child-bearing age at that time, so it's not implausible. To whom she was with child is not said.

Legend tells us that Ferrers's activities were not limited to her own lifetime. Her ghost has been seen in the vicinity of her old home, Markyate Cell, often galloping on a black horse with white flashes on its legs. In 1894, the then resident of Markyate Cell declared that he had often seen her ghost on the stairs of the house, where he would bid her a goodnight.

Another account tells of a workman on the bypass at Markyate who said that he was accompanied by a slim youth dressed in a long, dark coat and high, leather boots as he warmed himself at a fire. In a flash, the youth disappeared. A ghostly lady riding a ghostly horse has also been seen riding like fury on Nomansland Common, and there are tales of living horses being found in their fields in the mornings around the Markyate Cell area, the rumour being that they were ridden by a ghostly highwaywoman during the night.

The stories about the Wicked Lady, the moniker that Katherine Ferrers earned for her supposed crimes, probably have their beginnings in truth and have been heavily embroidered over the years as the reality has been obscured. It may well be that the Wicked Lady, as we now generally think of her, is a pastiche made up of a number of real episodes that happened to various people.

PATRICK FLEMMING

Birthdate Unknown • Died 1650

Patrick Flemming is often given the honour of having inspired the folk song, *Whiskey in the Jar*. He was certainly an Irishman and was born into a poor family in Athlone. His parents rented a small patch of land on which they attempted to grow and raise enough food to feed themselves and make money from the sale of anything left over. It was a meagre living and there was no chance of Patrick receiving the necessary education to help get him out of the social and economic situation into which he had been born.

Patrick displayed a lively character and this got him noticed by the Countess of Kildare who employed him, when he was 13, as a foot-boy. She was impressed with his natural quick-wittedness and paid for him to attend school. This, however, did not sit well with the youth, who refused to study, much to his mistress's dismay. His behaviour in general then deteriorated and he was finally dismissed from his post.

Instead of returning home to be a burden to his family, Patrick was lucky enough to get a job in the household of the Earl of Antrim. While his own peers didn't like his behaviour, Patrick seemed to find favour in his master, who continually forgave him for his misdeeds. That is, until Patrick went too far and made fun of the earl's resident priest. Flemming is supposed to have set the priest up to be caught in a compromising and embarrassing position, but the joke backfired and the earl, a serious Catholic, refused to believe the boy's story and had him thrown out of his employment for having made a mockery of the Church and its minister.

Flemming made sure he didn't leave empty handed; he took over £200 worth of goods and fled to Dublin. It was there that he fell in with a den of house-breakers with whom he worked for the next six years. During this time, he earned the reputation of being a dangerous criminal who was wanted for hanging. Very soon, in fact, he became too hot for Dublin to handle and, on leaving the city, he took to highway robbery.

Flemming worked a particular spot along the highway, near the Bog of Allen, and he robbed all and sundry who came along it. His technique was highly original; rather than announcing his intention to rob his victims, he would tell them that he was claiming the toll owed to him from those who passed across his rightful territory. He would then threaten any who demurred with instant death and he was not a man to make idle threats; he is supposed to have murdered several people during his reign of terror. By this time, Flemming had a sizable gang to help him control the area. These supporters were often caught and hanged for their offences, but Flemming seemed always able to avoid capture.

Many of his victims were wealthy or of high standing and included such people as the Bishop of Rapho and his travelling companion, the Archbishop of Armagh. Later, he took £1,000 from the Archbishop of Tuam. It could be seen that Partick Flemming, having developed a lifelong aversion to the clergy, deliberately targeted members of it to rob. However, he also held up Lady Baltimore and her 4-year-old son. The child was snatched from her and held as ransom for twenty-four hours while the poor woman found the price to pay for her son's life.

Either the pickings got slimmer or the travellers more wary, for Flemming was obliged to move to new territory and took to the roads around Munster for a while. It was here that he was caught when he tried to rob a gentleman of £250. Patrick Flemming ended up in Cork gaol awaiting his trial. It did not take this wily rogue long to figure out an escape route up the chimney.

Flemming evaded capture for several years after this and committed increasingly violent crimes. It is reported that he murdered five men, two women and a male youth during this

time, and badly disfigured Sir Donagh O'Brien by cutting off his nose, lips and ears during a robbery. But even the ruthless, daredevil and seemingly unstoppable Patrick Flemming came to a sticky end eventually. The landlord of the inn in which he was regularly drinking tipped off the authorities who ambushed the highwayman. When Flemming and his men reached for their arms they found that they'd been rendered useless; the thoughtful landlord had made sure that the guns were all wet so that the powder wouldn't go off.

Flemming, with fourteen of his men, was taken to Dublin, tried and hanged on Wednesday 24 April 1650. Afterwards, the dead highwayman's body was hung in chains on the main road out of Dublin as a warning to others of his ilk.

Flemming's dead body hanging in chains.

MARY FRITH (ALIAS MOLL CUTPURSE)

Born 1589 • Died 1663

Mary Frith, who came to be known as Moll Cutpurse, was a popular and colourful character both in her own lifetime and afterwards. Her main idiosyncrasy was that she always dressed in men's clothing and smoked a pipe. She acquired her moniker, Moll Cutpurse, because Moll was both a popular nickname for Mary and it was an often-used label for young women whose morals left a lot to be desired. Mary Frith fitted both these requirements. **Cutpurse** became her common surname because of her first and best-known activity: cutting the purse strings of unsuspecting victims.

Moll's eccentric lifestyle made her an ideal subject for fiction and she became the inspiration for a number of plays, ballads and novels. In 1662, John Day wrote the play *The Madde Pranckes of Mery Mall of the Bankside*, sadly now lost, and, in 1663, Thomas Middleton and Thomas Dekker wrote *The Roaring Girl*. *The Roaring Girl*'s title was taken from the term **roaring boys**. These were young men who frequented drinking places and houses of ill-repute, and who would finish their evening's entertainment by having very public fights among themselves.

Three years after Mary's death, an account of her life was written, *The Life of Mrs Mary Frith*. Needless to say, it was highly fictionalised. What is known, more or less, to be fact about Mary Frith/Moll Cutpurse is as follows.

Mary Frith was born in Aldersgate Street in 1589 to a reputable shoemaker and his wife. She was their only surviving child and was loved and cherished because of it. Every opportunity was taken by her parents to help her grow into a fine, gentle and decorous woman. However, Frith was a tomboy through and through and despised sewing and sitting still, wearing tiresome skirts and fiddly headdresses, and any other kind of female domestic duty or craft. She had few or no girlfriends, preferring the company of boys and playing boisterous games involving sticks as swords and other weapons. In fact, she gained a reputation at being an expert with the cudgel. Exasperated, Frith's parents finally turned to her uncle for help. He was a minister of the Church and not to be trifled with. He arranged for her to take passage to New England in an attempt to tame her spirit. Frith, however, jumped overboard before the ship left the harbour, swam ashore and went home.

Left to her own devices, Frith grew up without any intention of taking a position fitting her rank in society or one that would suit her limited formal education and domestic skills. In fact, at one stage, her father attempted to have her sent into service with a saddler. One account of her life says that her rebellion at this move and her refusal to comply led to her uncle's attempt to send her to the New World.

A young woman of Frith's station could well have turned to prostitution as a way of earning money, but she did not. From early in her adult life she started wearing men's clothes and using masculine mannerisms like smoking. She made no effort to be feminine in anyway and had no interest in being found attractive by men. Perhaps she had no natural inclination to fall in love with them. In one report she is said to have declared that she was not interested in sex for herself, at any rate. She also didn't like children and is not known to have ever had any.

One of her first attempts at making a living was as a fortune teller. She picked up the tricks of the trade from local practitioners and plied her skills with the best of them. Frith, now commonly known as Moll, did make a reasonable income from doing this, but she still spent more than she made and this led her to take up with the various thieves who frequented the taverns and other entertainment spots. Robbery of various kinds then became her staple method of getting money.

Over time, she had various stays in prison: Newgate, the compters and Old Bridewell.

To dress and behave like a man with no thought about its impropriety meant Frith enjoyed a freedom that none of her female contemporaries did. She even appeared on stage at the Fortune Theatre, a thing unheard of for a woman in her times. It is possible that acting in public was the reason that she found herself in trouble with the law for wearing men's clothes. She had to appear at the Court of Arches for the offence. Her punishment was to stand at St Paul's Cross during the sermon on Sunday morning wearing a white sheet. Frith was neither chastened nor embarrassed by this and as soon as her ordeal was over she immediately returned to wearing her own male clothing.

In 1614, Frith supposedly married Lewknor Markham, who may have been the son of the playwright Gervase Markham. It was obviously a marriage of convenience, giving Frith a married status that could be used in her defence when law suits were brought against her. There is no evidence that the marriage was anything more than a business contract.

Frith may not have been interested in participating in sexual activity herself, but it did not prevent her from acting as a pimp for other women. She had male and female clients, often finding suitable lovers for bored housewives. It is said that when these women died Frith would request donations from the woman's lover(s) to provide for any children left parentless. She told the men that the children may well be theirs.

After having spent numerous sessions in prison, she eventually decided that it was time to move on from her previous occupation and took to robbing on the highway. As a staunch Royalist, she made sure that she only held up Roundheads. Her downfall came when she attempted to rob General Fairfax on Hounslow Heath. She shot him in the arm and killed two of his horses to prevent further pursuit. Fairfax raised some soldiers in Hounslow to chase after her. Frith's horse gave out at Turnham Green and she was quickly over-taken, arrested and escorted to Newgate prison. With a bit of luck, however, and £2,000, she was able to pay off the injured party, receive a pardon and gain her freedom again.

There is a story that suggests she spent time in Bethlem Hospital, an asylum for the insane, for attacking General Fairfax and that she was released because she had been cured. If she *had* been an inmate of the asylum, it would prob-ably have had something to do with the bribe that she gave to Fairfax. Perhaps he agreed to a plea of insanity and then when she handed over the money she was pronounced cured.

Frith didn't return to highway robbery after this. Instead, she became a fence and broker for other thieves. Not only did she help sell on stolen goods for others, she was also known to help those robbed to find their missing watches and jewellery when they came, which they were bound to do because of her reputation as a fence. She charged a hefty fee for this service.

Such civic duty gave Frith the idea for another business enterprise: steal-ing fabric sample books from drapers and mercers and charging a significant fee for returning them again. By the time she was 74 she had been diag-nosed with dropsy,

Moll Cutpurse.

with her stomach and limbs swelling like balloons. In this condition, she made herself ready for death and paid for her funeral arrangements in advance. She refused to make a will, but distributed her money and personal affects to particular friends and relatives herself before her death.

It had been speculated that Frith was a hermaphrodite, but after her death this was found to be untrue; she was as female as she said she was.

Mary Frith was laid to rest in the churchyard of St Brigid's. There was a marble stone put at the head of her grave, which was engraved with an epitaph supposedly composed by John Milton. This would have made the old woman turn in her grave if it was true, as she had been an ardent Royalist and Milton was a sworn Parliamentarian. It is much more likely that it was written by someone trying to imitate Milton's style and perhaps trading on the reputation. Either way, it was destroyed in the Great Fire of London.

The epitaph is recorded to have appeared as follows:

Here lies, under this same marble,
Dust, for Time's last sieve to garble;
Dust, to perplex a Sadducee,
Whether to rise a He or She,
Or two in one, a single pair,
Nature's sport, and now her care.
For how she'll clothe it at last day,
Unless she sighs it all away;
Or where she'll place it, none can tell:
Some middle place 'twixt Heaven and hell
And well 'tis Purgatory's found,
Else she must hide her underground.
These reliques do deserve the doom,
Of that cheat Mahomet's fine tomb
For no communion she had,
Nor sorted with the good or bad;

That when the world shall be calcin'd,
And the mix'd mass of human kind
Shall sep'rate by that melting fire,
She'll stand alone and none come high her.
Reader, here she lies till then,
When, truly, you'll see her again.

GILDER-ROY

Born *c*. 1624 • Died 1658

Gilder-Roy was born into a wealthy Scottish family in Perthshire and became one of the nastiest criminals to rob on the highway. When he was 21 he came into his inheritance, which was his father's entire estate. However, it took him less than two years to lose it all through lavish spending. Once his land was sold, Gilder-Roy moved into his mother's little property and took whatever she had as his own. When she was finally sick of his bullying, taking from her and leaving the household without living expenses, she closed the purse strings tight. Gilder-Roy took his revenge by slitting his mother's throat while she slept, raping his sister and a maid, tying them up, looting the house and then setting fire to it. The two girls both died in the flames. It was a crime that horrified and disgusted the whole country.

Gilder-Roy, the chief suspect, fled to France. While on the Continent he supported himself through picking pockets, gambling, swindling and straight-out theiving. From France he went over to Spain and left a trail of notoriety behind him. After a three-year sojourn he finally went back to Scotland. The crimes had not been forgotten, but the search for the perpetrator had died down and other infamous criminals had taken his place at the top of the list for capture.

Gilder-Roy then gathered a band of willing followers to help him build a criminal empire around the counties of Athol, Lockable, Moray and Sutherland; remote places rather than heavily populated ones. He took on the persona of a robber baron, robbing the rich and exacting a heavy protection toll from the poorer folk in the form of cattle, food, drink, etc. He was likened to Robin Hood, only his motives and manners were very different.

The list of Gilder-Roy's victims is long and includes many well-known names of the day, Oliver Cromwell being one.

It isn't possible that all the crimes laid at Gilder-Roy's door were really committed by him or his gang, but their reputation was so vicious that they may as well have taken the blame for everything.

Eventually, three gang members were arrested, taken to Tolbooth in Edinburgh and sentenced to hang. They broke out and went into hiding, but were hanged when they were caught again soon after. Gilder-Roy, angry at losing three of his best men, held up the judge who had passed the sentence in order to get revenge and it was a brutal attack. The coachman and footmen were stripped, bound and thrown in a pond where they drowned. The horses were all shot and the coach ripped to pieces. The judge was then held in a wood until it was safe for his attackers to take him to the gallows, where Gilder-Roy's three men hung from the **gibbet**. The judge was strung up beside them and left to choke to death.

Soon after this heinous crime, a law was passed in the Scottish courts that a highwayman could be hanged as soon as he was captured. The trial and sentence would be made after the execution.

Gilder-Roy's reign of terror lasted too long and a proclamation was finally made, offering a reward for him alive or dead. In the end, it was his mistress, Peg Cunningham, greedy for the money, who told the officers that they would find him in her own bed. They quietly surrounded the building, but not quietly enough, because a slight noise alerted him to what had happened. Knowing it was Peg who had turned him in, he plunged a knife into her and savagely tore her body open. When the guards broke into the house to arrest him, Gilder-Roy fought savagely, killing a couple of the men. He was finally overpowered and taken to Edinburgh under heavy guard and manacled hand and foot.

Gilder-Roy was executed three days after capture in April 1658, without access to any religious rite. His body was left to rot on a **gibbet** between Edinburgh and Leith.

JAMES HARMAN

Born *c*. 1699 • Died 1725

James Harman's parents were quite well off (his father being a merchant in London), so he was another young man who could have had a long and successful life had he had a bit more go in him. In fact, he started reasonably; he did so well at school that when he was 14 he was enrolled in university. Here, he met with all sorts of young men, some dedicated to their studies and many others who were dedicated to having a good time, just as they are today. Consequently, he spent three years at university and achieved almost nothing except an enormous debt.

With little choice remaining, Harman's father bought him an **ensign**'s commission and he joined Jones's Regiment. He might have made a good army career for himself, but when the war with France ended the regiment was disbanded and Harman was left jobless. As with many in his position, Harman couldn't manage life as a civilian and racked up more debt without any means to pay it; he ended up in a debtors' prison. This was probably the last place he should have been placed as it meant that this weak-willed fellow came into contact with a whole manner of rogues putting suggestions of easy money into his head. One of these rogues was Lumley Davis, a young man of similar background to his own (see the entry for Lumley Davis).

Davis was released from prison by a friend who paid off all his debts and the prison fine. Harman must have also undergone a similar stroke of luck because he was released about the same time as his friend. They didn't meet up straightaway as Davis spent some time in hospital recuperating from an illness. Davis had been staying quietly at his friend's place in the country, but as soon as he could, he returned to London and sought out Harman.

When they met up they set about making plans for their future, deciding upon highway robbery as the easiest and most lucrative activity, but it didn't quite meet their expectations. Perhaps the inexperienced pair was inept or perhaps they had bad luck, but their first robbery was their only robbery. They took from John Nichols Esquire 1 guinea and 17s. They were soon caught and taken to Newgate to await trial for their crime.

Once sentenced to death, Harman made an effort to make peace with his God and prepare himself for death, repenting of his crimes and the fact that he had wasted so many great opportunities. Occasionally, he would talk with Davis. He and Davis were both hanged at Tyburn on 28 August 1724.

CAPTAIN JAMES HIND

Birthdate Unknown • Died 1652

James Hind had a fearsome reputation as being a ruthless highwayman, but the stories are always tempered with accounts of his fairness and kindness to the poor. Hind vowed he would never rob a poor person. Along with Claude Duval, James Hind is the archetypal, romantic, swashbuckling highwayman.

Hind was the only son of an Oxfordshire saddler. He was given a good education, learning reading, writing and arithmetic well enough to enable him to go into any business. When he turned 15, he was apprenticed to a butcher. However, he only stayed with his master for two years, partly because the man was very difficult to work for, but also because Hind wanted a more exciting life, he ran away. He told his parents that the master had been cruel to him and that he couldn't stay in his employment any longer, asking his gullible mother for money to help him find work in London.

When in London, Hind was immediately seduced by the attractions there: alcohol and women. One night he was out on the town with a young woman who had picked the pocket of a passing gentleman. Suddenly, she was arrested for the offence and, because Hind was in her company, he was arrested too and spent the night at the **Poultry Compter**. In the morning, he was released without charge as there was no evidence that he had been involved in the theft. The woman who had committed the crime was sent to Newgate.

During his evening in prison, Hind got to know the highwayman Thomas Allen who was also spending the night there on suspicion of a robbery – he too was released the following day. This was not a good friendship for Hind to make, as it led to the pair setting up business robbing on the highway.

Their first job together was at Shooters Hill. Allen let Hind show his mettle by keeping his distance from the action. Hind more than proved himself by robbing a gentleman of £15, although he gave him 20s of it back so that he could continue his journey without too much hardship. In relief at not having his head blown off, the gentleman stated that he would never give evidence against Hind. Allen was pleased with his apprentice's first robbery and they made a pact to support each other through any circumstances.

The two began their partnership just at the time Charles I was executed, and they swore an oath that they would not meet with any Roundhead on the road and let him live. True to their word, they reportedly held up Oliver Cromwell on his way from Huntingdon to London. The entourage consisted of seven men who quickly surrounded the two highwaymen as they stopped Cromwell's coach. In the skirmish, Thomas Allen was captured and taken to Newgate. He would be found guilty of trying to rob Cromwell on the highway and would hang for it.

Hind was able to escape. In fact, he supposedly rode his poor horse to death in his effort to outrun Cromwell's men. If he was to continue as a highwayman he would have to get another mount. This was easily and fortuitously done when he discovered a horse tied to a hedge, the owner out of sight. A brace of pistols hung from the saddle and Hind immediately leapt onto the horse, calling out that it was now his. Before he rode off, the real owner emerged from behind the hedge and yelled that it was not. Hind, sitting atop the horse with the pistols to hand, told him that he should be thankful that he only lost his horse and pistols and was left with his money to buy another one. In future, he was warned, it might turn out differently.

There is another story about how Hind procured a horse without paying for it. Whether it is another, separate instance or whether it is a different version of the first story isn't discussed. Whichever the case, the story went like this: Hind borrowed, for want of a better term, an old hack and set out into the countryside on it. He fell in with a gentleman on a fine horse and got into a conversation with him. Hind let the man boast about the talents of his horse and then persuaded him to demonstrate how it could jump over a hedge. When it did so, Hind asked if he could try it on the man's horse to see if it would perform as well for him. Gullible through vanity, the gentleman agreed. Hind and horse disappeared from view and the gentleman and tired old hack were left abandoned on the highway. Perhaps the truth behind the two stories is that the second version was the true one, but the gentleman, not wanting to appear the dupe he was, put a different version about. Interestingly, they both involve hedges.

James Hind, as has been noted, was a devoted Royalist and so when he met with Hugh Peters, a staunch Parliamentarian, he stopped him with a pistol to his head and demanded his money. Peters was not to be intimidated by the highwayman and began to spout biblical references about not stealing. Hind countered with his own biblical quotes about being loyal to one's king. The two adversaries exchanged a number of these passages until Hind put a stop to it by exclaiming that if the man didn't hand over his money he'd blow his brains out. This unmistakable phrase did the trick. Peters handed over 30 **broad pieces** of gold. However, Hind couldn't let the old man go without having the last word. He rode after him, quoting more scripture and procured the man's cloak by regaling him with, 'Our saviour has commanded that if any man take away thy cloak, thou must not refuse thy coat also.' Peters handed over his coat as well.

Peters, as a Presbyterian preacher, chose theft as the subject of the following Sunday's sermon. He chose text from Canticles, chapter five, verse three: 'I have put off my coat, how shall I put it on.' The story of Peters's robbery by Hinds had got around and a Royalist in the congregation only too happily shouted out that he should ask Captain Hind that question, which caused the whole congregation to burst into laughter.

Continuing his highway career, Hind met Sergeant Bradshaw on the road between Sherbourne and Shaftesbury in Dorsetshire. Bradshaw had been the judge who passed the sentence of death on the former King Charles I. Hind immediately knew who the passenger inside the coach was and not only showed no signs of intimidation when the man called out his name, but told him that he was a 'king-killing son of a whore'. He then stated that Bradshaw was in the same powerless position that Charles I had been when he stood trial. Hind would let him live, only so that he could suffer later at the hands of the hangman, on the condition that he hand over all of his money. Bradshaw produced 40*s*, but Hind was not satisfied and told him that he was going to blow his head off if the rest of the money wasn't handed over. A bag of **jacobuses** was brought forth and given to Hind.

Bradshaw's ordeal, however, was still far from over. Hind gave a long spiel about the glory of money and then told him that he and the other Parliamentarians, guilty of regicide, had gone on long enough glorying in their evil deed. How long they would remain exultant was another matter, but Hind would '... however, for this time, stop [his] race in a literal sense of the words'. He then shot all six of the coach horses dead.

Hind had a reputation as a hard and fierce highwayman, but he was also considered a fair one who would try to avoid bloodshed or violence, unless his victim had committed regicide. For example, he once stopped a coach full of young women who took him for a knight. When Hind realised this, he played along for the joke. He requested that he might borrow some money as he was in a desperate situation. The girls replied that they would have loved to help him, but the £3,000 that they carried was the dowry of one of them and they were on the way to meet the intended groom. Hind finally revealed himself as the notorious highwayman and said that he would not hurt the ladies, but he must have a third of the stash. When they realised that he wasn't going to take everything or kill them, the women handed over £1,000 with no more ado. Hind wished them a safe journey and congratulated the bride.

The story of the maiden going to her fiancé had, it is reported, a sad ending. In fact, if Hind had known about it, he would surely have taken out a fierce retribution on the young man. The girl told her betrothed what had happened to them on the road and he immediately told her that the marriage would be off unless her father could find another £1,000 to replace the loss. The girl's father had given everything he had to marry off his daughter and couldn't raise the extra money. The wedding was cancelled and the jilted bride died of a broken heart.

Anecdotes abound about Captain James Hind displaying the highwayman's cunning and bravery. One such amusing story demonstrates how he did not even need a horse to commit a successful highway robbery; he could have the victim stop at his very door. This story takes place at a time when Hind was very short of funds and without a suitable horse. He had taken a house that sat right beside the road running along the common. He then discovered that a well-known doctor would be passing by at a certain time on his return from receiving a hefty payment for a remedy that he had supplied. Hind stopped the doctor outside the house and begged him to come in to see his wife who was dying of flux. The doctor entered and went upstairs to attend the ill woman. Once inside the upstairs bedroom, Hind pulled out his pistol and introduced the doctor to his wife. Forty shillings were handed over without demur and Hind, locking the man in the room, said that he would leave him the house in recompense for his lost money.

Hind's goodwill towards those more unfortunate than himself is demonstrated in the story about the old man that Hind met on the highway, jogging along on an ass on his way to market. Hind rode along beside him and asked why he going to market. The man replied that he was going to buy a cow to give milk to his ten children. The man had saved up 40*s* over two years for this express purpose. Hind needed the money, but put forward a suggestion to the man that would see him double his money. Whether the man was gullible or whether he was afraid that his companion might harm him if he didn't comply with the request, he handed over the entire sum of 40*s*. Hind told him to meet him again at that spot in one week's time, swearing him to absolute secrecy.

We are not told how Hind accomplished it, but he returned as he promised, doubled the old man's money and added a further 20*s*.

Although Hind was known for his genteel ways and aversion to violence, he did once kill a man: a servant called George Sympson, who was riding in a great hurry to take a forgotten item to his master who had ridden ahead. Hind, in a nervous state of being pursued by the law, shot the man in the head because he suspected him of chasing after him and rode away as fast as he could.

Hind's next move was to join the rallying cry of the Royalists, who were trying to get Charles II onto the throne. The Battle of Worcester, where the Royalists and Parliamentarians met, was very bloody. The Royalists were defeated and Hind fled to London and hid in the house of Mr Denzle, a barber. While lying low and going under the name of Brown, Hind met an old acquaintance who reported him to the authorities. Hind was arrested and taken to Newgate prison. At his trial at the Old Bailey he was tried for several crimes. However, there was not enough evidence to hang him and Hind was transferred to Reading in Berkshire to stand trial for the murder of George Sympson who was from that county.

Hind was found guilty of the murder and would have been sentenced to death by hanging, but the following day he was granted a pardon, what is called an Act of Oblivion, for all his previous crimes including Sympson's murder. The pardon, however, was not what it appeared to be. It was a way of getting Hind to a place where he could be charged with high treason. Instead of the straightforward hanging he could have expected for murder or highway robbery, Hind now faced the gruesome penalty of being hanged, drawn and quartered. He was transferred from Reading to Worcester for the purpose.

At his time of execution, Hind declared that most of his victims had been members of the Parliamentarian party who had killed the rightful King of England and that his only regret was to die before seeing Charles II restored to the throne.

On 24 September 1652, James Hind was executed and his head set upon the Bridge Gate over the River Severn. A week later, it was taken down and buried, but the rest of his body was taken to the gates of the city and left there to rot.

CAPTAIN ZACHARY HOWARD

Born *c.* 1620 • Died 1652

Zachary Howard was born to inherit his father's estate in Gloucestershire. He had an excellent income and probably would have enjoyed it working his land if the Civil War hadn't intervened. Consequently, as a staunch Royalist, he mortgaged his land for a sum of £20,000 and used the money for the purpose of rallying men to fight in the name of King Charles I.

When the king was executed, Howard went into exile with Prince Charles, swearing an oath that he wouldn't suffer a regicide to live.

Howard eventually returned to England to fight at the Battle of Worcester when Charles II made an unsuccessful attempt to seize back his throne. He fought so well and bravely that is said that Charles himself congratulated him. The battle, however, was lost and Charles went back into exile. Howard stayed in his home country, even though he now had no land to call his own. Like so many men in similar circumstances, he then took to robbing on the highway to make ends meet. He, along with his brothers, tried not to rob any Royalist.

The list of victims of Howard's robberies is extensive and full of well-known Parliamentarian names. First on the list was the Earl of Essex, general-in-chief. The earl was travelling in his coach with a group of half a dozen of his own men as riding guards across Bagshot Heath. Howard was not deterred by the size of the band or the status of the passenger and rode to the coach door, demanding that he 'Stand and deliver!' or else have his head blown off. The earl didn't put up any resistance and handed over a bag of £1,200, which was probably revenue gathered from estates that had been seized from Royalists like Howard himself. The earl escaped with his life and a warning that they would meet again soon.

The next important target was the Earl of P– (name not given in full in *The Newgate Calendar*). Howard joined him as he and his footman rode on Newmarket Heath, engaging the earl in pleasant conversation, until they came to a deserted area. Suddenly, Howard pulled out his pistol and ordered the man to hand over his valuables or lose his life. Upon this unexpected declaration, the earl accused Howard of being a 'ranting Cavalier'. There followed a strong argument from both sides as to the worth of Oliver Cromwell. Howard ended it by shooting the earl's horse from under him and taking a purse full of **broad pieces** of gold and a diamond ring. To enhance the indignity, Howard bound the earl and his servant back to back on the one horse, with the earl facing backwards of course, and set the horse on its way with its hilarious cargo. The pair was a laughing stock when they reached the town, although the citizens untied them.

Howard then heard that the Earl of Essex's successor as general of the army, a man called Fairfax, had received some riches and was going to have them transferred to the house in which his wife was residing. Howard hatched a plan: he met up with the servant given the task of taking the wealth to his mistress and pretended to be a friendly traveller who shared the same political views as the servant. Not long before they reached the end of the ride, Howard revealed his true identity and, with pistol in hand, bade the servant hand over the valuables. The poor servant was outraged at having been duped by his new friend and blankly refused to hand over the goods. They began a hard fight in which Howard's horse was killed and then, in the course of the struggle, the servant was shot in the head. Howard quickly mounted the dead man's horse with its rich cargo and took off for Fairfax's house. Before he got there he dumped the bag of treasure in a hollow tree.

When he arrived at the house, he handed the mistress a letter that had been in the servant's coat pocket. It told the woman of her husband's success and gift that they'd been given from the mayor. Lady Fairfax asked where the gift was and Howard concocted a story of how he had left it with an honest innkeeper to avoid being robbed on the highway. The woman was impressed and had a bed prepared for the man that she thought was doing her a good turn. In the night, however, Howard crept out of his room, tied and gagged the servants and then did the same to the lady of the house and her daughter. Then, to his shame as a 'gentleman', he is supposed to have raped them both before stealing as much as he could from them.

The attack on the Fairfax household meant that a reward of £500 was offered for the capture of Captain Zachary Howard. Howard, in the meantime, had fled to Ireland. When Ireland was in full cry at the outrageous felonies of the man, he returned to Chester, England, while Cromwell was there, to put into action another daring plan against the Parliamentarians.

This time, Howard pretended to be a rich man getting ready to go abroad. He let it be known that he was a supporter of Cromwell and an anti-Royalist. Howard made such a good job of pretence that he came to be known to Cromwell personally and was often invited to dine with him. When the friendship seemed to be steady, Howard came to Cromwell's house early and surprised him in his bedroom, just as he was kneeling for prayers. Cromwell, suspecting nothing, invited his new friend to pray with him and Howard knelt beside him. But instead of putting his hands together and bowing his head, Howard pulled out his pistol, bashed Cromwell over the head with it and threatened to kill him, telling him that he was well prepared to hang for the offence.

Cromwell cowered on the floor and let Howard do and take what he liked. The first thing that the highwayman did was to bind and gag his enemy. He then searched the room for valuables and found 1,100 **jacobuses**. To finish the exercise, Howard dumped a full chamber pot over Cromwell's head and was well away before Cromwell could get anyone to hear him.

A week later, Howard wrote Cromwell a letter, jeering at him over the trick he had played as well as taunting him with his liberty.

Howard had perhaps laughed too soon because, not long after this, he tried to take on several Roundheads at once. Even though the Cavalier put up an astoundingly good fight, killing one man and wounding two others, he was captured and taken to Maidstone gaol.

Cromwell is supposed to have visited the prisoner in order to have the last say, but Howard returned as good as he got and his visitor did not get the pleasure he had expected out of the visit.

At the trial, Howard was found guilty of two rapes, two murders and a multitude of robberies. Although he pleaded guilty to all and confessed his regret for the murders, despite the fact they were committed against Roundheads, he declared that he would do it all again if he was given half a chance.

As the noose was lowered over his head, Howard stood defiantly, grinning at Oliver Cromwell to let him know who he thought the true winner was.

NATHANIEL JACKSON

Born *c*. 1692 • Died 1722

Nathaniel Jackson grew up not really knowing his father, who died when the boy was very young. He was, however, left in a comfortable financial position, his money appointed by a guardian, and was apprenticed to a silk weaver when he was a youth. Nathaniel ran away after three years of serving his apprenticeship because of the strictness that his master practised on him, and the fact that his allowance was kept to a minimum so that he wouldn't fritter it away. Gambling, drinking and engaging prostitutes were common temptations for young apprentices.

Nathaniel's guardian discovered that his charge had run from his apprenticeship and suggested he invest the rest of his inheritance in a modest dwelling. That way, he could live easily within his means and never have to practice a trade, but would be able to live on his late father's money. As with so many impatient young men for whom trade held no interest, Nathaniel ignored his guardian's advice, enlisted in the army instead and set off to Ireland with his regiment.

Nathaniel's biggest weakness was his fondness for women. In one case, this keenness led to a duel with a fellow soldier. Jackson was the stronger of the two and he gave the other man a severe belting. He eventually had to be dragged off by several officers and was consequently dismissed from the army.

With nothing else in mind to occupy him, Jackson went back to his guardian, but his respite didn't last long and boredom drove him to seek excitement and pleasure. He then spent an intensive few months living a dissipated life until he was advised by a friend to take a break for the good of his health and pocket, not to mention his damaged, corrupted soul. The outcome of this advice was to drive the young man to London with their blessing and many presents of money to help set him up there. However, it did not take him long to get through what he'd been given and he did not spend it on the basic necessities of living. Inevitably, Jackson soon had to start making money for himself. It was at this point that he fell in with a couple of old friends from Ireland, John Morphew and a man by the name of O'Brian.

From there, O'Brian instigated their first, and for Jackson his last, highway robbery. They robbed a man near Hampstead. He had little money and no jewellery, so the trio took his coat, waistcoat, two shirts and a hairpiece. O'Brian was set to kill the poor man after this pathetic robbery, but Jackson and Morphew pulled him away.

Jackson, being the inexperienced and gormless criminal, was discovered and arrested as the culprit for the crime. O'Brian got wind of the arrest and fled to Ireland.

As he awaited his death, Jackson resigned himself to it and went without fuss to the gallows on 18 July 1722.

JAMES LEONARD

Born *c*. 1675 • Died 1693

James Leonard had been in the army for just a few years, probably as a waiting-boy, certainly not as a soldier, before he took to the highway. When he was caught, he boasted that he had committed a good many robberies; quite a feat for an 18-year-old.

On his way to the gallows, he pulled out a knife and tried to cut one of the ropes that was to be used for the hanging. When asked why, he told his guards that it was only so they'd have to buy a new rope. The knife was so blunt, however, that it made no impression on the rope.

As he was mounting the scaffold he told the audience that the weather was so cold they had no need to hang a man to get rid of him; he was in more danger of freezing to death.

JOHN LEVEE

Birthdate Unknown • Date of Death Unknown
Lived in the time of Joseph 'Blueskin' Blake

John Levee's father was French and came to England with Charles II at the Restoration. He taught French to the children of courtiers and the bastard children of the king himself. He did not teach at court, but kept a boarding school at Pall Mall. The school was prosperous and when Levee Senior had made a comfortable sum to retire from teaching, he set himself up as a wine merchant. He built himself a sizable income in his new trade and gave his own children an expensive education.

In common with so many good things, the wine merchant's business eventually came to a bad end. When it failed, John Levee's father abandoned his family in England and went to Holland. Instead of following on from his first-rate education, John Junior was thrown upon the charity of the French Society. They looked about for a suitable apprenticeship for him, but finally settled on sending him to sea in a man-of-war. He actually did well in this state, but when he returned home he was encouraged to train as an accountant. Levee knew that he should have stayed in the navy, but peace had come and there was not much in the way of employment.

Accountancy was certainly not the answer for Levee, who enjoyed the outdoors and high adventure. Consequently, he and several of his friends set themselves up as highwaymen. They offered no violence, however, and would simply stick a hat into the coach and ask for donations. They always gracefully accepted what they were given and did not ask for more than that. It was more a form of begging than robbing.

Things changed somewhat in the modus operandi of the robbing when Levee joined up with John Blake, known as Blueskin. When they robbed a coach in which a woman was carrying a basket of cakes, Levee helped himself to a couple of them, but Blueskin tried to search her for money. The woman fought back, scratching and hitting. They then left her alone to continue her journey.

Blueskin's influence affected Levee greatly; Blueskin would stop a coach and demand them to 'Stand and deliver!' or he'd shoot them, and it was not long before Levee was copying his friend's words and actions. The longer he stayed with Blueskin's gang, the more his manner towards his victims deteriorated.

On robbing a coach in which the passenger made a small show of resistance, Levee and Blueskin took his great coat as a form of punishment. The pair of highwaymen may well have done more to the man they'd robbed, but their activity was spoiled by another coach coming their way. Levee thought that he knew some of the passengers on it and made haste to disappear before he could be identified.

Levee and Blueskin, accompanied by some of their gang, also stopped the coach of the same Mr Young who was robbed by John Molon and James Carrick (this unfortunate gentleman must have been an easy target for highwaymen). During this attack it was Levee who entered the vehicle and took from the gentlemen their watches, money and other goods. Apparently, both Levee and his victims remained calm and polite to one another.

On the same night as they held up Mr Young and his friends, Levee, Blueskin and the gang also came across an old man riding a horse. The gang pulled him from his mount and searched him for money. They found 2*s*. The gang members wanted to give the man a beating, but Levee intervened and persuaded them to put him back on his horse complete with his 2*s*.

The only documented case of Levee actually using violence against a victim was when one of them, a man called Betts, whacked him over the head several times. Levee lashed out with the butt of his pistol and unfortunately knocked out the man's eye.

Four of the gang were arrested after the Young robbery: Levee, Flood, Oakey and Blake. Blake won his freedom when he gave evidence against his former companions. Levee, Flood and Oakey were sentenced to death. The actual date of his death is not recorded, but he was 27 when he died.

JAMES LITTLE

Birth Date Unknown • Death Date Unknown
Lived and died in the first quarter of the eighteenth century

This young man had a very ordinary upbringing. He was taught reading, writing and the basics for a variety of jobs and decided, when he was old enough, that he would like to follow in his father's footsteps and be a painter (of walls and houses, not pictures). Little was not bad at his job and earned a good rate for his labour. It did not, however, agree with his temperament and he often abandoned work in favour of drinking with his mates.

Little was eventually seduced into becoming a highwayman by one of his so-called friends, a soldier. While Little was drunk, the man got him to agree to accompany him immediately on a robbery. He accosted the first travellers to come along, pulled out his pistols and threatened to shoot them if they didn't hand over their goods. Yet Little lived up to his name and was of small use to the soldier or the victims of his friend's robbery. The boy was very drunk and could hardly stand up. This was probably just as well, as the soldier was caught not long after and hanged. Little was arrested at the same time, but was not indicted as he bore witness against the soldier.

Instead of being chastened by his friend's grisly end, Little took himself off in search of adventure. He then made the acquaintance of the famous highwayman John Shepherd's friends (especially the female ones) and was inspired by their incessant talk of Shepherd's bravery to act out similar crimes.

James Little, however, didn't get the chance to perfect his technique. He performed just one successful robbery on a Mr Evans, who lost £20, some keys and his walking cane. His next attempt was to be his last and it was made against Lionel Mills. Little made him hand over three keys (curious items to steal unless he also had an address to go with them), a hand-kerchief and 16s: hardly a magnificent haul. Little then tried to pull a turnover from around the man's neck. He didn't succeed in this theft, although he nearly choked the man to death. Unfortunately for Little, he didn't kill Mills. The wounded man chased the boy until he caught and apprehended him.

James Little was tried and convicted of both crimes and sentenced to death. He was a mere 17 years old.

THOMAS MALORY

Born *c*. 1405 • Died 1471

Sir Thomas Malory is more famous for writing *Le Morte d'Arthur*, the epic tale of chivalry and the search for the Holy Grail, than highway robbery. However, there is speculation about which Thomas Malory truly was the author of the Arthurian legends.

In the book printed by William Caxton, the printer has punctuated *Le Morte d'Arthur* with his own cryptic messages to the reader: 'For this was written by a knight prisoner Thomas Malleorre, that God send him good recovery.' Then, 'And I pray for you all that readeth this tale to pray for him that this wrote, that God send him good deliverance soon and hastily.'

At the end of the book, Caxton says of the author Thomas Malleorre, 'As Jesu be his help.' The last insertion is supposedly authorial and begs the reader to pray for the author while he is alive and then when he is dead.

Out of the six contenders for the real Malory, there is one particular favourite amongst scholars and that is Sir Thomas Malory of Newbold Revel, who was a soldier. In 1443, this Malory was arrested with Eustace Barnaby for kidnap and theft to the value of £40 from a Thomas Smythe. The charges were not pursued and Malory was set free.

Later in the same year, he was elected to Parliament and put in charge of distributing funds to poor towns in Warwickshire. Obviously, no one believed him guilty of the original theft or they wouldn't have trusted him with such an important job, handling money.

Over the next seven or eight years, Malory was accused of many more offences. The list of crimes he is supposed to have committed, along with his gang, were numerous, brutal and included rape as well as robbery.

Malory's claim to fame as a highwayman rests on his supposed encounter with Humphrey Stafford, the Duke of Buckingham. Malory, working with a gang, had held up the duke and demanded money with menaces. The result of the robbery is not specified and it is not known if it was even successful. It was never brought to court and may be nothing but rumour.

By 1452, Malory was locked up in Marshalsea prison on a variety of serious charges. He refused to plead guilty to any of them and ordered a re-trial with a new jury made up of men from his own area. Malory was not retried, but released instead. His freedom, however, was short lived as he was arrested for a new offence in March of the same year. Either Thomas was an industrious thief or he was being framed. On this occasion, he managed to escape after bribing the guards, but was caught and put back inside in a matter of weeks.

Bail of £200 was posted in May and Malory was again a free man. Why they let him out on bail is a mystery, as the authorities were soon on the lookout for him again. They couldn't find him, however, because he was already back in gaol in Colchester, awaiting trial for more of the same: highway robbery and theft involving horses. Malory's purse must have been well lined because he was able to escape again and stay at liberty until the end of the year.

For several years after this, Malory spent a lot of time in one prison or another. At one point, he was in the debtors' prison for defaulting on loan repayments, owed for all the bail that he had paid out.

The last that was heard of this Thomas Malory's criminal life was the pardon he was granted by Edward IV when he gained the throne.

He died on 14 March 1470 and is buried at Christ Church in Greyfriars, not far from his one-time popular resort of Newgate prison.

WILLIAM MARPLE & TIMOTHY COTTON

Marple: Born *c*. 1699 • Died 1729
Cotton: Born *c*. 1704 • Died 1729

William Marple and Timothy Cotton both came from caring backgrounds and received decent educations. However, while they had been to the same school, become friends and received the same education (incidentally, this is the same school that I attended), Marple came from a well-off family, while Cotton's was quite poor.

As they were approaching adulthood, Marple tried three different trades before settling on joinery, although he didn't see his apprenticeship out, and Cotton trained as a poulterer. Marple then went on to marry the woman he adored, who was peaceful and industrious. His life changed at this point and he gave up his restlessness to settle down to hard work in order to make a comfortable home for his wife. Cotton, although married, continued to enjoy the company of prostitutes and began to spend his hard earnings on showering them with gifts that he couldn't afford.

Tragedy struck when Marple's young wife died and, distraught, he gave up work and settled into a dissipated life instead. When his grief had abated for his wife, he took up with a young woman who drained him of all his finances by wanting extravagant luxuries. His solution was to turn to highway robbery.

At first, he acted alone. He robbed without discrimination, poor and rich alike, and is said to have been one of the most prolific highway robbers working at the time. It's not clear when Cotton joined his old school mate on the road, but when he did they became a nasty pair of thieves. For example, in their first robbery they targeted a woman who sold joints of meat. First, they took a leg of mutton for their own dinner then they demanded her money. When she refused, they searched her until they found 7*s*. Marple hit the woman to teach her a lesson for lying to them.

The second highway robbery that Marple and Cotton committed together was on Hampstead Road when they held up a coach and threatened the passengers, but they were interrupted in the middle of the robbery by three mounted men. Marple raised his pistol and warned them to back off. The men didn't understand what Marple said and rode towards him, putting their hands in their pockets in order to hand over their valuables. Marple repeated his order and the second time the men turned about and rode off in a hurry. The passengers were relieved of their possessions and Marple and Cotton fled the scene.

Their third and final robbery was on a man called Stout who was a servant of a Captain Trevor. They stole his hat, 2lbs of butter, his belt buckle and a few pence. In fact, it was what you'd call slim pickings. It was for this robbery that they were finally caught and sent to the Old Bailey for trial. The sentence was hanging for both of them.

Cotton committed five robberies in all, three of them with his schoolfriend. Marple, on the other hand, had been working so hard as to notch up thirty or forty robberies; at some time between the death of his wife and working with Cotton, Marple had fallen in with a very bad crowd, including a woman who had been Jack Shepherd's mistress, Elizabeth Lion. Eventually, he found the woman so detestable that he dumped her and the rest of the gang. After this, he married again: a decent young woman just as his first wife had been. She had no idea what her husband did for a living.

William Marple showed signs of sincere remorse for his crimes while he was waiting to hang. He confessed to more crimes than he'd been charged with and claimed that he'd been drawn into robbery as a means to support his habit of indulging in the company of undesirable women, but he had never been a drinker or a gambler. If this is true then we are

177

left to wonder why Marple continued to rob when he found a decent wife and remarried again.

Cotton also appeared to be deeply sorry for all the pain and distress that he'd caused his victims and his own family, and also insisted that his wife knew nothing of his criminal activities.

William Marple and his old friend Timothy Cotton were hanged at Tyburn on 24 March 1729.

JOHN MOLONY

Birthdate Unknown • Died 1722

John Molony was born in Dublin and went to sea as soon as he was old enough. His trustworthiness was first called into question when he and a number of his fellow sailors were called to account over the loss of the ship on which they were travelling in the Mediterranean. There was a suggestion of foul play, but nothing came of the enquiry and Molony continued to work at sea. He was a good sailor and enjoyed his profession, but once ashore he would rapidly fritter away his money on the usual pleasures: drinking, gaming and prostitutes.

He returned to England after a harrowing trip to Sicily, where he witnessed an appalling murder of a woman by her husband and the attempted murder of another woman, all in a jealous mistake. Whether this haunted him is impossible to say, but it did nothing to adhere him to the ideals of marriage and a conventional life. Molony hit the gaming table hard when he got ashore and was constantly in need of funds. It was at one of these places that he met James Carrick and Daniel Carroll, and the three of them decided to become a gang of highwaymen.

What followed was a robbery committed against a Mr Young, which got Molony and Carrick arrested. Carroll fled to Ireland. The convicted pair, however, appeared to use their trial as a platform for displaying their wit at the expense of their victim, Mr Young. When the sentence of death was handed down, Molony had at least sobered up enough to admit remorse for his behaviour.

He and Carrick were executed on 18 July 1722.

THOMAS POLSON (ALIAS HITCHEN)

Born *c.* 1697 • Died 1730

Even as a boy at school, Thomas Polson displayed all of the attributes that would lead him to a life of crime: laziness and a total disregard for the learning process. He found it very hard to learn to read or write (something that he might have been able to be overcome in modern times, with willing parents and lots of good luck) and, as he would obviously never make a scholar, he was taught husbandry by his father in the hope that he would be a reputable farmer.

When Polson was 20, his father settled him with £20 per annum, a good farm and a charming wife with a nice little dowry. Perhaps this was all too easy and there was not enough challenge to lift Thomas out of his complacency; perhaps he was sick of an overbearing father who left him with no control over his own life. Whatever the reason, Polson began gambling in a serious way. The money was soon gone and the farm neglected. Polson had no money left, but a wife to look after. Instead of altering his behaviour, he decided to begin to take what he wanted from other people who had what he didn't.

Polson's first victim was his own father and the theft was blamed on a maid who worked for the family. It wasn't until six months after the event that Polson's father decided to have the girl arrested. When hearing what was about to happen, Polson wrote to his father confessing to the crime and asking that the girl be pardoned and her good name restored. Polson's father was an honest and decent man and did both of these things. From then on, relations were very strained between father and son, although they eventually mended when Polson promised to become a good and honest, hard-working citizen. This resolve, however, did not last long and soon Polson was on his way to Wales to steal horses.

The first horse taken was sold to a London butcher for £16, although it was a good horse and worth a lot more as a riding animal. When the money had all been spent, Polson took himself off to Wales again, this time to rob people of their money.

His first robbery was of a gentleman with whom he made friends at an inn. They were both drinking and Polson made sure that his companion got quite drunk and then promised he'd get him a woman to keep him company in bed. Polson instead robbed the man of £6 and took off before the other was awake in the morning.

Polson's wanderings took him to Canterbury and then all over Kent, but he was unable to make much money from his acts of highway robbery. In fact, in Maidstone he helped himself to ten linen shirts hanging on a hedge to dry. The haul of shirts brought him £5 in London when he sold them to a Life Guardsman.

From London, Polson went to Norfolk where he settled down for a while before he began robbing again. This was a deliberate plan so that the people of the area wouldn't suspect him, the newcomer, as being the perpetrator of the thefts. To make himself seem even more innocent and inoffensive, Polson pretended to be lame. Once he was accepted into the community, he began his robbing in earnest. The first thing he did was steal a mare from Sir John Habbard (later the Right Honourable Lord Blickling). This was almost the last crime he committed; he was seen, identified almost immediately and forced to ride off at a great pace, taking back roads in order to shake off his followers. Having ridden to London, Polson tried to sell the horse at the Haymarket, but news had carried fast and the theft was already being talked about. He didn't risk trying to sell her. In the end, he left her at an inn as security for the loan of 4 guineas from the innkeeper.

At this point, Polson's father wrote to him offering not only forgiveness but financial help if he would only leave off his life of crime and settle down to honest work. Polson decided he'd give it a go; after all, he wasn't doing very well in his career of choice. The resolution to be honest didn't last; money was not coming in any faster and the lifestyle was tedious. Slipping into his old ways, he helped himself to a horse from his brother's stable and set off on the highway again. His destination was Wales, as it had been the first time he went on the road. The pattern seemed to be to gravitate between Wales to London. London was the place of entertainment where he could lose his hard-earned money. From London, after his money was gone, he'd go back into the country to get some more.

Polson may not have been a violent robber, but he was not particularly courteous or charitable either; his first victim was an old man in Flintshire who had only £5 or so and a silver watch. Polson stole them without hesitation and took off as fast as he could.

After this, he went to Doncaster and robbed an old farmer, taking 40s and the man's horse. Polson stopped 15 miles from his attack and set the horse free to return, if it could or would, to its master. He then continued on foot all the way home to Shropshire. He stole from other travellers the whole way, but never managed to get a decent amount of money for all the pains and risks he took. (It is interesting that quite a number of Polson's victims were old men, perhaps this was coincidence rather than design.)

After this last adventure, which neither paid off nor proved exciting, Polson tried again to settle to his father's routine, only stealing every now and then to keep his hand in; he was fond of mutton and this was his object of choice to thieve. It was clear that he was never going to make it as an honest farmer; his wanderlust was too great, and again, after a few months of trying to be a settled husband, he took off after having a bad argument with his wife. This time he headed to Yorkshire rather than Wales.

On this trip he proved as inefficient at theft as ever and, at one point, was reduced to nicking the sheets off the bed at the inn. Yorkshire was hopeless. London at least held variety and interest; it was back to London.

Settling himself in Leather Lane, Holborn, Polson took a long hard look at his achievements. The conclusions he came to were rather grim: no money, no friends, a family with whom he fought and no aptitude for making money in any form whatsoever. He then made the decision to head for Hampstead, the Mecca for all highwaymen.

He made three visits to Hampstead before he was finally able to complete a successful robbery. His victim was yet another old man in a chaise who came across his path. Polson managed to rob him of 6 guineas, a watch and a mourning ring. After robbing the old man, he holed up in the inn pretending he was sick in case a description of his likeness was circulating the streets (his general inefficiency could, in fact, have been caused by this kind of overly cautious approach to his profession). When he discovered that it wasn't, he ventured forth and tried two consecutive weeks of robbing.

Although his labours were not always successful, he stuck it out because he had heard a rumour that an old man was going to be travelling that way soon carrying over £800. Polson, who was always so careful, became impatient waiting for the promised haul and went for the next traveller that passed his haunt instead. This was the downfall. The man he attacked, Mr Thomas Andrews, was no feeble old fellow, but a man who was able to chase after him, catch him and take him into custody.

This was the end. Polson was sentenced to death and he resigned himself to it. He wrote to his parents, apologising for his behaviour and acknowledging their wisdom with regards to the plans they had made for his life. He mentioned he'd written to his wife a week before, but had not heard back from her. He regretted leaving his wife in such disgraceful circumstances and hoped that she and the children would manage to live well. The letter was signed, 'Your Dying Son.'

Thomas Polson was hanged on 7 October 1730.

TOM ROWLAND

Born *c*. 1654 • Died 1699

We have already heard the stories of women who took to the highway dressed in breeches and cloaks, tricorn hats and masks, but this is the story in reverse.

Tom Rowland was a Hertfordshire boy who served out his apprenticeship to a bricklayer. There is little to tell about the robberies that he committed or with whom he associated, but we know he enjoyed the good life and didn't want to work for it in the conventional way.

His long highway career began when he stole a horse from the Duke of Beaufort in Gloucestershire, and he made a living in this way for eighteen years: an exceptionally long time for a highwayman. His secret was to dress in women's clothes and sit side-saddle when committing a robbery, but swing his leg round and sit astride when he had to make a quick getaway. Even this clever disguise didn't prevent Rowland from eventually getting caught and sentenced to hang, however.

On the day of his execution, instead of the prescribed prayers or confession before a priest, Rowland spent the time with a young woman from the prison who needed money. Needless to say that what they got up to was thought to be offensive.

Rowland was hanged on 24 October 1699.

Tom Rowland robbing a coach.

FERDINANDO SHRIMPTON

Born *c.* 1700 • Died 1730

Apparently, Shrimpton was the son of a famous highwayman who had been based in Bristol. No one who knew the father suspected him of anything, however, as he always presented himself as being very respectable and honest. The double life he led came out one night when he was drinking at an inn when some constables entered. Shrimpton Senior thought they were after him (although, it later turned out that they were looking for someone else), drew his pistols in panic and shot one of the men dead. It was for this murder that he was arrested, later convicted and sentenced to hang. While in prison in Bristol he confessed to a whole list of other offences. He was hanged and then his remains were hung in chains outside the city as a deterrent to others who might try his trade.

The young Shrimpton served as a soldier for some years before taking to the highway in his father's footsteps, and teaming up with his cousin, William Shrimpton, and Robert Drummond. Hounslow Heath was one of their favourite haunts and it is estimated the trio could do as many hold-ups as ten per night. It was during one of these robberies that Ferdinando shot and killed the coachman of Mr Tyson. When the three of them were finally apprehended, William Shrimpton turned evidence against his former mates.

While in gaol awaiting execution, one of Shrimpton's victims came to them to see if he could get his horse and watch back. In order to get the information, he had to pay the villains 1 guinea. The horse was easily recovered, but the watch was more difficult as Shrimpton didn't want to get the pawnbroker into trouble or, more likely, he didn't want more evidence appearing. Finally, when the ordinary who took down the account of Shrimpton's crimes appealed to the robber, Shrimpton got his wife to retrieve the watch.

According to one account of their time in gaol, neither Shrimpton nor Drummond appeared remorseful for any of their crimes, not even the murder of the coachman. When they approached the gallows, the men were apparently joking and chatting amongst themselves as if nothing unusual was going to happen. The ordinary of Newgate contradicts this account. The account claims that their actions were, in fact, the complete opposite of the description; Shrimpton, especially, showed signs of illness and needed his wife to help him walk.

Shrimpton was hanged at Tyburn on 17 February 1730.

JOHN SMITH

Born *c.* 1681 • Died 1704

I have included Mr Smith in this list of highwaymen and women, not for his courtesy or courage, but because of the shortness of his highway-robbing career and his lack of motivation to run away.

John Smith was an educated Winchcomb man from a respectable and comfortable family. He completed an apprenticeship as a **peruke** maker and then promptly went to sea in search of adventure and fortune. It is doubtful that he found either, as he returned to land as soon as he could.

On his return, Smith met another **peruke** maker in Chancery Lane, who was obviously not making much money at his trade because he suggested that they try their hands at highway robbery. Smith readily agreed and they settled for their first try the following Sunday.

Smith almost didn't go through with the plan. He noticed the gallows at Tyburn looming over him and he got very cold feet, having a premonition that that would be where he was going to end his days. But his companion wasn't to be talked out of it and told Smith that hanging wasn't such a bad thing; everyone had to die at some point.

Their first robbery was of a grey mare from a Mr William Birch. On the following Monday morning, Smith set off on the mare by himself in the direction of Epping Forest with the intention of making a real go of his new activity. He encountered three stagecoaches and held up each one.

Tuesday, he either took the day off or didn't confess to any robberies, because there is no record of any being made that day.

Wednesday was busy with the robbery of another three stagecoaches and a hackney coach, all on Hounslow Heath.

Thursday and Friday are not accounted for, but Smith robbed another three stagecoaches at St Albans on the Saturday. From the whole adventure, however, he only made £20.

His last robbery was made the following Monday; he held up the coach of Thomas Woodcock and robbed Mrs Woodcock of 4 guineas, two keys and a silk purse. This final robbery was witnessed by a gentleman and his servant who were out riding. They chased Smith on horseback into Colefall Wood and it wasn't long before they came across the villain with his horse tied to a tree. The gentleman sent his servant off to get back-up. A group of men then came to help search for the robber, but it didn't take long to find him lying under a tree and making no attempt to escape.

When one of the men threatened him with a **blunderbuss**, Smith called out not to shoot and discharged his own pistols into the air. He was hauled up off the ground and taken off to Muswell Hill. The evidence of his highway activities was in his pockets: a mask, powder and shot and some of the stolen money. He was asked why he hadn't tried to escape and he replied that his horse was no good, so he didn't bother. It sounds rather that a guilty conscience or an internal inertia prevented him as much as a dud horse.

John Smith, wig-maker and inept highwayman, was hanged at Tyburn on 20 December 1704.

ROBERT SMITH

Birthdate Unknown • Died 1803

Robert Smith put a slightly different slant on the art of highway robbery. Having no horse of his own with which to hold up coaches and get the occupants to 'Stand and deliver!', he would hail a handsome cab and give directions to be driven to some place outside the town. When the coast was clear and there was no danger of being disturbed, Smith would halt the coach and then rob the driver. This is not dissimilar to robberies performed on modern-day cab drivers.

The Newgate Calendar gives a very short career span for Robert Smith, telling us that he began this mode of robbery early in March 1803 and was executed on 8 June of the same year.

The first known instance of Smith's innovative form of highway robbery was when he engaged a handsome cab at ten o'clock one night in early March at Charing Cross. Smith presented himself as a gentleman and asked to be taken to St John's Farm on the Edgware Road. As they neared the address, Smith asked for them to stop, saying that he thought they had passed the house. When Smith put his hand into his pocket, on the pretence of getting out his purse, he produced a pistol instead and threatened to shoot the driver dead if he didn't hand over his day's earnings. The coachman readily complied with his demands. Smith then took the man's watch as well and took off across country.

Not long afterwards, on the evening of Monday 6 March, Robert Smith, again purporting to be a gentleman, took another coach, this time to St George's Row on the Uxbridge Road. Smith threatened the cab driver with death if he didn't hand over his money and poked him in the ribs with a **tuck-stick**, which injured the man. Smith ran off shouting that he'd shoot him if he pursued him.

Whether it was bad luck or bad management is unknown, but this highwayman's line of business came to an abrupt halt on a night two weeks later. Smith was strolling along the King's Road on a Sunday night when he was stopped by a patrol. They questioned him, but received only vague and unsatisfactory answers as to his activities in the area at that time of day. The patrolman then found that Smith was carrying a pistol in the breast of his coat. This was enough to warrant his arrest and the case was investigated the next day at Bow Street.

Once in custody, it was discovered that Smith was not such a clever fence as he was robber. He had pawned the first coachman's watch at a local shop and kept the ticket for it. The watch, identified by its true owner, and the finding of the pawn ticket on the prisoner, meant that Smith was charged as guilty. Not only had he made the mistake of keeping incriminating evidence against himself once, but he did the same thing to another coachman and had kept the ticket for that pawned object as well. Added to this were other charges of robbery and one of inflicting a wound with a **tuck-stick**.

With such damning evidence and the testimony of at least four victims, Smith could do nothing but plead guilty to all of the offences. In a last, desperate bid to keep his life, he asked for mercy in the light of it being his first offence. This did nothing, as the magistrate pointed out that there were five other impeachments against him and that there was also one of actually shooting at someone whom he had tried to rob.

The sentence, therefore, was hanging and it was carried out on 8 June 1803 in the Old Bailey, outside the debtors' door.

WILLIAM SPERRY

Born 1702 • Died 1725

William Sperry and his younger brother accepted the seemingly generous offer of transport to the plantations in America in return for a period of seven years, in which time they both worked for a plantation owner. In reality, it was not a good proposition for the boys, as the work they were expected to do was hard and the treatment they received from their master was harsh and sometimes cruel. Perhaps the situation was not that different from those desperate people these days who are lured to first-world countries with the promise of good jobs and incomes and then find themselves in slave conditions.

Sperry at least served out his term and, on his release, went to Philadelphia and found employment and lodgings with a family of Quakers. He attempted to improve his reading and writing and was given help and encouragement from his employer. Sperry put his heart and soul into these activities, something which he also applied to his religious studies. Quakerism surrounded him and there was pressure for him to convert, but he remained staunchly loyal to the Church of England and would regularly travel 5 miles to attend his own church.

From Philadelphia, Sperry decided to take to the water and got work on a trading ship, travelling around the American coast. On one of these trading runs the ship was attacked and taken over by pirates. The pirate captain was Edward Low, who had built a notorious reputation for brutality. Sperry was invited to leave his position as captive and join them as a pirate, but he declined on the grounds of his deep religious belief and its attendant morals. One of the young man's traits was deep honesty and when he felt compelled to tell Low that his crew were making mutinous plans, Low had him put ashore on the Leeward Islands.

Sperry then enlisted with the English navy and set sail on a man-of-war whose job it was to seek out and eradicate the pirate menace in the area. Sperry witnessed the trial and execution of a band of pirates while in the navy's service. Only five of the men escaped death and that was because they had not joined the pirate crew of their own free will, but had been forced into it in much the same way as he had been by Edward Low. Perhaps this sparked a sense of empathy with them.

Sperry had left England as a youth, but returned as a grown man. Shortly afterwards, he married a young woman whom he did not have the means of keeping in a style suited to her desires; he had no skills to fall back on for life on shore in England. Inevitably, and in spite of his supposed moral beliefs, it didn't take him long to begin a life as a highwayman. His favourite haunts were Hampstead, Islington and Marylebone, where he became well known as someone to avoid.

Sperry soon became involved with a criminal gang who were not just involved in highway robbery; they would stoop to pickpocketing, fraud and blackmail, amongst other things. One of their favourite targets for robbery was the gambler, and they used inside information to get tips about who was worth robbing. On one such occasion, a well-known gamester tried to bluff his way out of being robbed of his substantial winnings. He almost succeeded, but the most experienced robber of the gang told him that they knew for a fact that he had won a lot more than he claimed; if they didn't find it on him they would cut him open and find it inside him. The money was produced very quickly from under the man's arm and the gang ran off without further ado.

The same night, as the gang members were on their way home, they encountered a coach being driven by a gentleman. Two members of the gang approached the coach on either side and grabbed hold of the horses. The driver, however, whipped the horses so that the robbers were dragged along the ground and the coach was able to drive off without being robbed.

By the time Sperry made his last robbery he was on his own and apparently desperate. His intended victim, Thomas Golding, claimed to have no money on him and Sperry, therefore, demanded all of his clothes. He was caught for this crime and taken to gaol to await trial. He was subsequently found guilty and sentenced to hang. He then confessed to all the crimes he had committed and acknowledged that his punishment was fair.

He was hanged at Tyburn on 24 May 1725.

DICK TURPIN

Born *c*. 1705 • Died 1739

Dick Turpin is one of the most famous names in the history of highway robbery. However, from near-contemporary accounts, such as a broadsheet published in June 1737, it is rather difficult to see how he achieved the romantic status that he has enjoyed almost since his death. From the recounts of his exploits, as recorded by the ordinary of Newgate, he seems to have been anything but gallant and was, at times, involved in cases involving rape, torture and murder.

William Henry Ainsworth, a nineteenth-century writer, is largely responsible for the rise of Turpin as a folk hero. Ainsworth's material probably came from stories, often in ballad form, that had arisen surrounding Turpin from the beginning of the century.

A hundred years before Ainsworth, Richard Bayes's *The Genuine History of the Life of Richard Turpin* was offered for public consumption shortly after the trial. This kind of sensationalist work, purportedly offering the facts about notorious criminals, was the result of an almost insatiable demand on the part of the general public and the resulting publications often contained more fiction than anything else.

Rookwood, Ainsworth's novel, was written in 1834 and, while Turpin was not the main subject of the story, his character was portrayed in such a lively and attractive manner that he captured the public's attention. The episode in the book that really shot Turpin to top of the charts was his remarkable and frankly unachievable ride from London to York in a single day. Unfortunately, poor old Black Bess, Turpin's trusty mare, dropped dead after the event, the effort proving too great a strain on the faithful animal. This story was so well liked that it appeared as an excerpt on its own, published as a penny dreadful, *Black Bess or the Knight of the Road*.

Dick Turpin riding Black Bess.

The real story of Dick Turpin is buried deeply under all the glamorous myths. It is impossible to unearth it all, but we will attempt to see some of the unattractive possibilities of this man.

There is no definitive birthdate for Turpin, but his baptism is recorded as having taken place on 21 September 1705, where he was named Richard Turpin, soon shortened to 'Dick'. It is stated in some sources (specifically in the transcript of Turpin's trial by Thomas Kyll) that he was born at the Blue Bell Inn, later named the Rose and Crown, in Hempstead, Essex to John Turpin and Mary Elizabeth Parmenter, who were the owners of the inn.

Although it is said he was the landlord of the Bell Inn, John Turpin was a butcher by trade, and it is thought that Dick, the second youngest of six children, followed his father into the trade, having been apprenticed to a butcher in Whitechapel. He then opened his own shop either in Thaxted or at Buckhurst Hill, Essex. Prior to running his own butchery, he married Elizabeth Millington in 1725; this is the woman that the researcher Derek Barlow (1973) thinks is the most likely candidate for Turpin's wife. Richard Bayes, the contemporary biographer of Turpin, however, says that Turpin married the daughter of a man called Palmer.

According to Bayes, Turpin made a sincere attempt to make a living as a butcher, but was hampered in his enterprise by the fact that he had no credit in the markets and had not had time to build up a relationship of trust with his would-be creditors. To help his cash flow, Turpin is said to have stolen a neighbour's livestock, which he butchered on his own premises to sell in his shop. The neighbour had suspicions about the young butcher and instigated an investigation that looked pretty damning for Turpin. When the authorities went to arrest him, Turpin jumped out of a window and got his wife to dispose of any incriminating evidence, such as the carcasses of the beasts that were claimed to have been seen at his premises. He avoided prosecution at this time. From cattle stealer to smuggler, Turpin joined a gang of smugglers and made a nice living out of it for a while. Yet fortune turned, and he was no longer able to follow his new profession.

Another suggestion for the start of Turpin's life of crime is that he was trading in deer meat that had been poached from the Royal Forest of Waltham. The young butcher's suppliers were the Essex gang, also known as the Gregory Gang after its founding member, Samuel Gregory, and his brothers, Jasper and Jeremiah. The gang also included Joseph Rose, Mary Brazier, John Jones, Thomas Rowden and John Wheeler. Bayes says that the gang expanded its activities under Turpin's direction, suggesting that they try their hands at house breaking. It is not confirmed if Turpin was involved in these more aggressive activities, but there is a possibility he was.

The gang began their activities with a spate of attacks. They robbed Peter Split, chandler and grocer (also referred to as Peter Strype by Bayes), in his own home; Richard Woolridge of Woodford who was a furnisher of small arms in the office of ordnance at the Tower of London; John Gladwin, **higler**; and then shortly after, Ambrose Skinner, an elderly farmer.

The following February, 1735, two nasty attacks on separate households were perpetrated by members of the gang. Turpin was said to be present at both of them. The first was a raid on an elderly widow. Bayes quotes Turpin as yelling at her, 'G-d d—n your blood, you old b---h, if you won't tell us, I'll set your bare a—e on the grate.'[1]

When the widow refused to give up her gold, the gang did just that until the woman could hold out no longer and told them where she'd hidden it.

Turpin and the gang went on to carry out another vicious attack; this time on an old farmer and his servants. The man was made to sit on the fire without any pants on while kettles of water were poured over his head. He was then beaten about the head and body with pistols. The account also mentions Samuel Gregory raping one of the maids.

After one more sadistic attack on a farm in Marylebone by Turpin's gang, the Duke of Newcastle put up a reward of £50 that would lead to the capture of the villains. Added to this was an incentive for the criminals to report each other. Bayes notes that in the *Gazette* there appeared an advertisement offering a pardon to any of the gang who would give evidence against any of his friends who had been directly involved in the activities of rape, assault or robbery.

No one was caught immediately and the spate of brutal robberies continued until the gang, thinking themselves safe from discovery, were carousing at a tavern. Officers, working on a tip-off, surprised them; Fielder, Saunders and Wheeler were arrested and taken off for trial along with a couple of their female companions. Wheeler, the youngest, possibly only 15, was easily persuaded to give evidence against his companions and received a pardon for doing so. Fielders and Saunders were hanged. Wheeler also gave a detailed

---

1 Bayes, Richard, *The Genuine History of the Life of Richard Turpin*, (D'Anvers Head, Chancery Lane, London: J Standen, 1739), p. 5.

description of Turpin, naming him as a butcher and telling them that he wore a **natural wig**.

While Turpin continued to roam free, most of the other gang members were finally rounded up and imprisoned. Some died of illness in gaol, others were executed and Mary Brazier, one of the gang's fences, was transported to the Thirteen Colonies.

Alone after the disastrous dispersion of his gang, Turpin swore to be his own man and never become involved in a gang again. The resolution was held until he tried to hold up another notorious highwayman, Matthew King. Turpin wanted the man's fine horse and, not knowing him as a highwayman, began to ride alongside him making polite conversation. At a quiet spot in the road, Bayes' biography records that Turpin pulled a pistol on King and told him to hand over his goods or receive a bullet in the head. King laughed and said, 'What! Dog eat dog? Come, come brother Turpin, if you don't know me, I know you and should be glad of your company.'

Barlow (1973) tells of a companion Turpin had before meeting with King, probably a man called Thomas Rowden and known as The Pewterer. Turpin and this companion committed several robberies but Rowden was taken in July 1736 on a charge of counterfeiting and was transported.

In Bayes' account, no mention of Rowden is made. He says that Turpin and King made a home in a cave hidden amongst trees between Loughton Road and King's Oak Road. Apparently Turpin's wife would visit her husband there, often bringing food for the men.

James Sharpe, in his book *The Myth of the English Highwayman* (2005), suggests that, before Turpin took up with King, he may have spent time abroad, possibly in Holland as there was too much interest in having him arrested.

Turpin work with Matthew King for some time before they were joined by a third party: Stephen Potter. The company came to its sticky end, however, sometime around May 1737.

It started with a horse being stolen by one of the trio from a Joseph Major, who reported the theft. Intelligence came to the landlord of the Green Man in Leytonstone, who happened to be none other than Richard Bayes, Turpin's biographer-in-waiting. (Perhaps giving his version of events more credence than any other, as Bayes would have been a witness to the events of that night.)

Bayes went to look at the stolen horse that had been left at the Red-Lyon Inn in Whitechapel and decided to stick around to see who would come to collect the animal. The man who finally appeared was John King, Matthew's brother. John King tried to talk his way out of any involvement in the theft, claiming he had bought it legitimately. When he realised the ruse wouldn't work and on threat of being charged with the theft himself, he gave a description of his brother.

Bayes heroically tackled King and in the struggle King's pistol flashed in the pan, meaning it didn't go off properly. King called out to Turpin, waiting to one side on horseback, to shoot the man. Turpin fired as he was directed by his friend, but missed Bayes and shot King instead.

Matthew King lived for a week after receiving the shot and Bayes says that he called Turpin a coward for leaving him alone at the mercy of the law. Barlow, however, offers several other descriptions of the events; he says that even Turpin didn't agree with Bayes. The newspapers were later to report that it was Bayes who fired the fatal shot.

Turpin was forced to flee after this and went to Epping Forest. When he was seen and recognised by Thomas Morris, one of the innkeeper's servants, Turpin shot him dead.

Turpin then changed his name to John Palmer and under this alias went to Yorkshire and then Lincolnshire. He took on the persona of a horse-trading gentleman and socialised with others of that standing. What happened next is still a bit of a mystery. We know he shot the rooster belonging to his landlord. The act was witnessed by Mr Hall, a neighbour, and reported to the owner. The incensed landlord then went to Justice Crowley for a warrant for 'Palmer's' arrest. The Justices of the East Riding of Yorkshire then asked Palmer to supply them with sureties of good behaviour, which Palmer refused to do, and he was taken to the Beverly House of Correction.

During Palmer's stay in this establishment, an inquiry was made into how he made his money. When it was mentioned that he travelled a lot, often with different sets of horses, it was suspected that he might be a horse thief. On further investigation, it was decided that Palmer was too dangerous to be held at Beverly House and was transported to York castle instead.

Palmer had been in York castle for four months when it was finally discovered that he was none other than Dick Turpin the highwayman. The discovery was made when Palmer wrote to his sister's husband for aid in the matter of the horse theft. When the letter arrived at the brother-in-law's local post office he refused to pay the postage for it because he claimed he didn't know anyone in York. He may have suspected that it was from Turpin and didn't want to be linked to him more than he could avoid. The letter ended up in the hands of the man who taught Dick Turpin to read and write and he identified the handwriting. The old man then went all the way to York castle to identify his former pupil as Richard Turpin.

John Turpin, Dick's father, wrote to him in prison saying that he was trying hard to have the sentence transmuted to transportation and that if he had the money he would willingly give it to help him.

Turpin's trial was transcribed in court by Thomas Kyll, professor of shorthand. The charge was horse theft, a serious offence that carried the death sentence. It was complicated and witnesses were called from around the country. The jury eventually found Turpin guilty as charged and the sentence was hanging. Who knows how long he might have gone on 'horse trading' if he hadn't shot his landlord's rooster in public?

York didn't have an employed hangman, but used a system where a prisoner, if he volunteered for the task, would receive a full pardon for acting as executioner. Turpin's hangman was a fellow highwayman called Thomas Hadfield.

Turpin was taken to the gallows in York by open cart, accompanied by his hired mourners, and climbed the ladder to the scaffold. The noose was put over his head and then he jumped from the ladder to be hanged by the neck until he was dead. This was called the short drop method and meant slow strangulation. For this reason, the bodies were left hanging for several hours to ensure that they really had suffocated.

Turpin was buried the next day at St George's church graveyard. His body was apparently stolen that night by body snatchers, but the thieves were caught with the cadaver and it was re-interred.

Turpin certainly led an exciting life if the accounts are true, and many of them probably are, even if they have been heavily embroidered. The notion of him being a gentleman rogue though is difficult to understand, except for the fact that later versions about his exploits were pure fiction. At his best, Turpin was a horse thief and at his worst, a murderer and a colluder in brutal assaults.

WILLIAM WALKER

Birthdate Unknown • Died 1807

William Walker was indicted for highway robbery, but whether he had made a full career out of it isn't known. There are also questions surrounding who the real victim in the case actually was: the old man Walker was accused of robbing or Walker himself.

The old man, one Thomas Oldfield, may have been an aged fellow, but apparently he was not frail or helpless. He was walking across the countryside from Pentonville to the town on 10 October 1807 at ten o'clock at night when he met a man who asked him if he had any money, which hardly comes in the same class as 'Stand and deliver!'. Oldfield demanded to know why the other wanted to know and, seeing that the old man was obviously not the charitable type, Walker then demanded the money. The old man handed over a grand total of 7*d*, but as Walker took it in his hand, Oldfield gave him a whack in the side and sent him staggering. Walker tried to draw his weapon, but Oldfield was again too quick for him and punched him in the face, which knocked Walker off his feet. Oldfield then leapt onto the prone man and began hitting him. They thrashed it out for several minutes until Walker begged the other to let him get up. Oldfield assented but only on the condition that Walker hand over the bayonet he was carrying.

When they were both on their feet, Oldfield threatened to run Walker through with his own bayonet if he came any closer. Walker then took no time in escaping with his 7*d*.

Oldfield's son then appeared on the scene and was told by his father, 'That scoundrel has robbed me, and probably would have done me some mischief had I not overpowered him!' Unfortunately for Walker, the matter did not end there and the bayonet was used as evidence against him. It turned out that he was a serving soldier and he was confronted with it the next day after attending parade with a puffed-up face and numerous cuts and bruises, looking very much the worse for wear.

Walker could not or would not offer a proper defence against the charges and was sentenced to death on being found guilty. At the last minute, however, Oldfield stepped in and requested Walker be spared the death penalty. Consequently, Walker was instead ordered to leave the country and never return.

Though it can only be conjectured that this was an isolated case of robbery, and may not have even been planned as one (is it too much to think that Walker was only going to ask to borrow or even beg for some money?) it seems that Walker was as much a victim as Oldfield was.

NED WICKS

Born *c.* 1683 • Died 1713

Ned Wicks had been given a very sound education by his parents, who owned an inn at Coventry, in the hope that he'd settle down to a respectable profession, such as becoming a clerk. Unfortunately, Wicks found this position a trifle underwhelming and, after just over a year of working as an excise man, he threw it all in to build a career upon the highway.

Wicks made at least two successful robberies before he was caught during a third near Croydon. He ended up in the Marshalsea in Southwark, but he had friends who were more than willing to pay up the money that he'd taken during the third robbery and double it.

Having such a close shave with the law and facing the prospect of execution for his crimes did not deter Wicks, who was soon back to his old tricks on the highway. This time he teamed up with Joe Johnson, who also went under the alias Sanders. The two performed a number of robberies together until one fateful day when Sanders was shot and badly wounded, and Wicks made his escape without a backward look. Sanders was taken to Newgate, charged with the offence of stealing one Mr Woolly's watch and money and hanged at Tyburn on 17 February 1705. He was all of 22 years old. Wicks outlived his companion by another eight years.

Following Sanders's death, one of Wicks's noted exploits occurred on the highway between Windsor and Colebrook. He held up the coach of a lord and demanded money. Instead of ready compliance under the threat of death, Wicks was met with a display of bravado by the lord, who told Wicks he'd have to fight him for it. Wicks was keen to take the challenger on, but the lord, seeing his assailant so willing, withdrew his challenge, and broke out in a fit of swearing.

Wicks, obviously impressed by his victim's expletives, challenged him instead to a swearing match; the groom was to be the judge and the wager was 100 guineas, 50 from each party. The pair swore solidly for fifteen minutes before the groom announced Wicks the winner, but he congratulated his master on having sworn admirably for a man of his social standing. Whether Wicks would have let the lord take the money if he had won the bet is rather debatable; perhaps he would have had to hold him up again.

In 1713, when Wicks was nearly 30, he was finally caught again; this time for a robbery committed in Warwickshire. He was taken to Newgate, found guilty and sentenced to death by hanging. His parents petitioned hard for a more lenient sentence, but to no avail and he was executed on 29 August 1713.

JAMES WRIGHT

Born *c.* 1687 • Died 1721

James Wright was born in Enfield. He was apprenticed to a **peruke** maker, served his full apprenticeship, then set up business in the Old Bailey. In common with many young men before him, Wright found the delights of the city too attractive and his income wasn't anywhere near enough to pay for them. There was no other option than to go robbing on the highway.

James was another of those criminals who refused to hurt his victims and made numerous attempts to quit his new trade. He tended to target rich travellers rather than poor because he felt they could afford the loss. This would also lessen his own feeling of guilt when he robbed them.

He was a careful criminal, but even the most careful can find themselves in prison, which is just what happened to Wright. By some chance of pure good luck, however, he was acquitted of the charges against him and walked free.

Thanking his guardian angel profusely, Wright then swore that he would stop his thieving ways. A friend took him to his house in the country to keep him away from the temptations of the city and the angel must have thought that the job was done. It was not to be; an old companion of Wright's reported him to the authorities for another matter and then gave evidence against him. There was no reprieve the second time; the sentence was death.

Wright appeared truly repentant of his crimes. In fact, he was only a half-hearted highwayman to begin with, and it is said that when he robbed someone he did it with tears in his eyes. He also refused to give the names of any of his gang members, saying that he hoped they had reformed themselves and would live better lives because of it.

He was hanged at Tyburn on 22 December 1721.

JOHN YOUNG

Born 1691 • Died 1730

John Young was born to a gardener in Kensington who gave his son a reasonable education for one of his station. Young did well at school and seemed set to build himself an honest and profitable life. He even got to choose an apprenticeship for himself in coach building. Unfortunately, it was either the wrong choice or the wrong master, because he ended up despising his work and walking out.

In order to support himself, Young then tried his hand at being a hackney coachman. His fellow coachmen trained him up and helped him find regular employment. Driving appeared to agree with him and he did very well at it, getting a position with a Mr Blunt in Piccadilly. He built an excellent reputation as an honest and reliable employee and, with a good reference in hand, became coachman to a gentleman and his family. He managed to save up a sizable amount of money while working for them.

His next step was to find a suitable wife, which he did in the form of a lady from a good family in Kentish Town who brought with her a dowry. Young then decided that his financial situation would allow him to live as a gentleman and there was no need to take on outside employment.

Although Young's savings had seemed considerable, it didn't take long to use them up on general living expenses and he was obliged to find a new source of income. Instead of returning to the trade he knew well, driving a coach, he set up as an innkeeper and bought the King's Arms in Red Lion Street. It was a success and within five years was set to become a lucrative business. Young, however, was not happy there and tended to spend money as soon as it was made.

It is possible that his wife had died during this time and this had affected him. Whatever the cause, he ended up in Ireland, alone, and it was here he began his life of crime, defrauding people of their money. Ireland lost its attraction when people got wise of his reputation and avoided having any dealings with him. Young was forced to return home to England.

On his return, Young's family wanted nothing to do with him, but he took no time in finding a mate in a woman who had once been cook to a bishop and his family. When she and Young married she brought to their union a nice amount of money and valuable goods. Unfortunately, Young had got into the habit of frittering away his money and soon got through his new wife's.

He then took a job as a revenue officer, surveying candles. Not surprisingly, he didn't last a year in this position and it was left to his wife to help support them. This led him to take to robbing on the highway to seek financial independence from his wife.

His first robbery was quite successful, he got 15 guineas out of it, but was so frightened of being discovered that he fled to Bristol. When all possibility of pursuit had died down, he gained confidence and decided to go back to London.

On the way, Young travelled with a man who couldn't help talking about a sum of money he had recently come into and which he was carrying with him. When they were in an isolated spot, Young made the man strip and hand over his money and any other valuables. By accident, Young's pistol discharged and the victim was badly wounded. Young left the man to his fate, which he assumed would be death, and raced off to avoid any implication in the crime.

Young, afraid of what he had done, was determined to leave the area and go to the west of England. Before he did so, he saw an article about his murder of the young traveller in the paper. He immediately went home to tell his wife that he needed to leave town because he was implicated in something that could lose him his life, but he did not tell her the facts of the matter and let her conjecture on the nature of the problem, never guessing that her husband was actually a murderer. She was sympathetic and gave him her own savings (she was working as a cook again in her husband's absence).

Young took lodgings at Horsely Downs, close enough for his wife to visit him weekly and supply him with money. One morning, she brought him a considerable sum, which made him very suspicious of how she came about it, but he didn't let it stop him from accepting it or questioning her about it.

His hiding place was eventually revealed and he discovered that the man he thought he had killed had actually survived. The man was able to have him arrested and taken to the New Gaol. His wife was arrested not long afterwards for robbing her mistress of 100 guineas. She ended up in Newgate prison.

The victim of Young's serious assault, Thomas Stinton, recovered enough to testify against Young and the jury had no trouble in finding Young guilty of all charges.

Young's wife gave an account of the robbery with which she was charged, which differed greatly from her husband's. She claimed that it was he who robbed her mistress when he visited his wife at her employment. She may well have been an accessory to the robbery because she went into hiding the afternoon it was committed, appearing again when Young had been arrested. She was sentenced to transportation for her theft.

John Young showed all the signs of repentance for his crimes, becoming religiously devout as his death approached. In this state, he received his old father and they were reconciled to each other.

Young was executed on 1 June 1730.

MARY YOUNG (ALIAS JENNY DIVER)

Born *c*. 1700 • Died 1741

In common with many of the highwaymen and highway-women mentioned in this book, Mary Young didn't limit herself to one form of criminal activity, but was expert in several. She received her nickname, Jenny Diver, from her dexterity as a **diver**. Diving being the popular title given to pickpocketing.

Young was the illegitimate daughter of a woman called Harriet who, until her disgrace and subsequent dismissal, had been a lady's maid in Ireland. Harriet had her child while she was living in a brothel, the only shelter she could find in her circumstances. The young mother couldn't care properly for her daughter (either couldn't or wouldn't because of the stigma of being unmarried) and abandoned Young to a series of foster homes.

When she was 10, Young found a permanent home with an old lady who made sure the child was taught reading, writing, arithmetic and to sew a fine seam. She was a quick and able student at all of these lessons and decided that she would try becoming a seamstress in London.

Young then persuaded her lover to help her find the money for her fare to England, promising to marry him if he did. The young man found the money readily enough by robbing his master of 80 guineas. He and Young embarked as soon as they could.

Once in England, the couple took lodgings in Liverpool until they could travel to London. Apparently, Young had been very seasick on the voyage over and needed time to recover her energy. In the short time they were there, however, her companion was arrested for his thefts in Ireland and was sent back to stand trial. His death sentence was reduced to one of transportation. Young was good enough to send him his belongings and some money before she took the coach to London.

As for Young's ambitions to become a professional seamstress, they had soon disappeared when she found herself in the company of a girl called Anne Murphy, who was also from Ireland. Anne was a pickpocket who associated with other pickpockets and she soon had Young initiated into the gang. Before she was allowed to do any robbing herself, she was taken along on expeditions to observe how it was done. While she was in this trainee's state, she was given a small sum of money on which to live. Young proved very adept at the activity and soon excelled even Anne's dexterity. In fact, she became so proficient that she ended up heading the gang under her new moniker of Jenny Diver.

Jenny Diver.

Diver, as she was known from this time on, had a number of devices she used for diverting attention from her activities. She could slip a ring off a finger when she was shaking a hand; she'd feign illness and slip her fingers into pockets while concerned people were offering her smelling salts; it is even said that in church she would wear a false set of arms which lay docilely in her lap while her real ones were hard at work around her.

Diver successfully made her living in this way until she was into her 30s. In 1733, she was caught picking a gentleman's pocket and was sentenced to transportation to Virginia for seven years. When she embarked on the ship that was to take her to America, she had been able to arrange for a number of comforts to be put on board for her. She was also able, with her wealth, to arrange a fairly comfortable lifestyle for herself once out in the colonies; there would be no harsh labouring under a hot sun for Jenny Diver!

In common with a number of criminals who had been sent abroad in this way, Diver could not settle to a new life in Virginia; she couldn't even complete her sentence and returned to England well before her seven years were up, which was a capital offence.

Once home in London, she resumed her old living of pickpocketing, cut-pursing and highway robbery and, at the age of 38, she was again apprehended along with two male companions. She did not, however, admit to having been arrested, tried and sentenced previously. She worked and lived under a number of aliases and the name she gave for this crime was Jane Webb. As there were no records of a Jane Webb having been caught stealing before, Diver was given another sentence of transportation. Apparently, the newspapers knew that Jane Webb was actually Jenny Diver and reported at the time, but it made no difference to her sentence and she was sent off to America.

Twelve months later, Jenny Diver was back in London and took up where she'd left off as if she'd never been away. Her old gang was no longer around and she set up in business with Elizabeth Davies and a man whose name is not known. They established a pattern whereby the male member of the trio would offer assistance to ladies as they attempted to cross a mounted, wooden walkway. As they were concentrating on their balance and the gentleman's attentions, Diver and Davies would be slipping their hands in and out of pockets. It was during one of these sessions that a woman caught Diver in the act, grabbed hold of her and called to people around her to get help.

The charge was highway robbery for both women, but their companion was not apprehended. Diver was also charged with having returned from transportation. She was unable to fall back on a false name this time as she had been recognised as the person who had been sentenced once before for theft. They were both sentenced to death by hanging.

Davies's sentence was reduced to transportation, but Diver's was unchangeable even though she claimed she was pregnant (when she was examined this was found to be false). There was no way that she could lie or buy her way out of the death sentence, so she turned to her original Christian faith to help her face it.

Jenny Diver was hanged at Tyburn on 18 March 1741. Her body was buried at St Pancras churchyard.

PART 3

FICTIONAL HIGHWAYMEN AND HIGHWAYWOMEN

A highwayman came riding.

It could be said that much of what appears in this book is fictional. Rogues like Dick Turpin have been turned into characters in plays and novels so that little of the real men are left. During and after Turpin's trial and execution, the public were mad for stories like his. They wanted sensational murders and <u>daring</u> escapades. This insatiable appetite was fed with broadsheets covering the latest criminal events, and even ballads were composed about them.

John Gay wrote *The Beggar's Opera* in response to something Jonathon Wild mentioned to Alexander Pope. Wild asked what Pope thought of a pastoral opera performed by the inmates of Newgate prison. Gay took the opportunity to write a satirical work inspired by criminals like Wild himself. One of the characters is a highwayman by the name of Macheath who heads a gang of villains.

John Gay also wrote a ballad based on Joseph Blake, known as Blueskin, telling of his attack on Jonathon Wild.

Scene from The Beggar's Opera *after Hogarth.*

The ballad appears in a play by Jon Thurmond called *The Harlequin Sheppard*.

Alfred Noyes's highwayman (from the poem, *The Highwayman*) was indeed a gallant and courageous man, which is more than can be said of the rogue in *The Highwayman Outwitted*. In this ballad, the highwayman is outwitted by a young girl that he attempts to rob on her way to market. If she had been a rich lady the ballad may have had a different outcome. The young farmer's daughter is told to strip naked and hand over all her money, but she doesn't let her situation make her a victim and she quickly mounts the highwayman's horse and takes off for home, complete with his saddle bags full of gold coins.

In the ballad *The Female Highwayman Priscilla*, a young woman dresses up like a man and rides out on a summer's day. She sees her sweetheart on the road and in true highwayman tradition bids him to 'Stand and deliver!'. This is an interesting version of the tested-lover type of ballad. Usually it is a young man, in disguise, who tests his sweetheart's fidelity by pretending that her lover is dead but that the girl can have him, the bringer of the bad news, instead (it is amazing that the girls never recognise their boyfriends under the disguise or that they always fall into their lover's arms when the disguise is uncovered instead of giving them a mouthful for being so cruel).

In this song, however, it is the girl who disguises herself in men's clothes, sees her lover on the highway and bids him 'Stand and deliver!', which he does. After robbing him of most of his valuables she then challenges him to hand over his diamond ring. Heroically the young man refuses to hand over the ring, declaring that he'd rather die as it was given to him by the woman he loves best in all the world. The supposed highwayman doesn't shoot him, but rides away. When the two lovers meet again, the young woman out of her disguise and dressed as herself, the young man notices his watch pinned to her dress, the same watch that the highwayman had relieved him of. At his puzzled expression the girl confesses to her trick and tells him it was to test his love. In the notes to this ballad, it is suggested that it comes from the mid-eighteenth century, when highwaymen were all the rage.

Leon Garfield is a twentieth-century novelist who sets a lot of his works in the mid- to late eighteenth century, with some of the stories involving highwaymen. One of Garfield's villains, Black Jack, inserts a sort of metal pipe into his throat before hanging; this prevents his windpipe closing and choking him to death. He revives after he is cut down. A similar device is used by John Masefield for his protagonist in his book, *Dead Ned*. Whether it was something that was actually done hasn't been mentioned amongst the documents that I have read.

GLOSSARY

blunderbuss: a gun with a barrel that is longer than a pistol, but shorter than a rifle. It has a large muzzle and shoots an assortment of projectiles. It works on the **flintlock** system.

bob wig: a short, neat wig worn by older men and some tradesmen.

broad pieces: gold coins in denominations of 23*s* or 25*s*.

chucks (also called jackstones, jacks, knucklebones): small stones or knuckle bones from sheep, which are thrown into the air to be caught, often on the back of the hand.

cutpurse: the name given to a thief who uses a small knife to slit the strings of a person's purse as they walk by.

diver: a pickpocket.

ensign: a junior rank of commissioned officer. In infantry regiments the ensign traditionally carried the flag from which he took his title.

flintlock: a mechanism for triggering the spark that will ignite the powder and make the ball shoot out of the muzzle of the gun.

gibbet: a device for executing criminals. Gibbet can refer to a guillotine, scaffold or even an executioner's block. It is also used to describe an iron cage in which executed crimnals were hung in a public display as a deterrent to others.

higler or higgler: door-to-door salesman.

Jacobite: a supporter of the Jacobite rebellion, which wanted to see Stuart kings back on the English, Scottish and Irish thrones.

jacobus: a coin from the reign of James I worth 25*s* at the time.

mantua maker: a bespoke dressmaker for males or females.

moidore: Portuguese or Brazilian coin worth about 27*s*. In use from 1640–1732.

musket: a rifle working on the **flintlock** system.

natural wig: a long, full wig of real hair made to look like a person's own hair.

peruke: a man's wig.

postilion: a rider who rode one of the horses pulling a vehicle. Usually, there was no coachman if there were postilion riders.

Poultry Compter: a small prison, or compter, run by the Sheriff of the City of London. It got its name from the location in which it was set up, near the poultry produce area of Cheapside in London. The compter was the early equivalent of a low-security gaol. It was for holding debtors, vagrants, religious dissenters, homosexuals, prostitutes and drunks.

roaring boys: young men who partake in public brawling.

snuff: powdered tobacco leaves that are kept in a small elegant box and taken out in pinches to be inhaled through the nose.

snuff box: a decorative case for housing **snuff**; they could be very beautifully made and encrusted with precious stones.

span-farthing (also called span-feather and pitching pennies): a game played in the street with counters, pennies or small stones. The first player throws the counter on the ground. The second player has to try to hit or toss his counter as close as possible. If the player can span the gap between the counters then he has won, otherwise his counter becomes the target for the next player to hit.

tie wig: a medium-length wig with enough hair at the back to be pulled into a loose pony tail and tied with a bow.

tuck-stick: a sword stick.

BIBLIOGRAPHY

Hayward, A.L. (ed.), *Lives Of The Most Remarkable Criminals: Who have been Condemned and Executed for Murder, the Highway, Housebreaking, Street Robberies, Coining or other offences*, Collected from Original Papers and Authentic Memoirs, Gutenberg project, *www.gutenberg.org*.

Proceedings of the Old Bailey, London's Criminal Court 1674–1913, *www.oldbaileyonline.org*.

Ashton, J., *Eighteenth Century Waifs* (London: Hurst and Blackett, 1887).

Burgess, C.F. (ed.), *The Letters of John Gay* (Oxford: Oxford at the Clarendon Press, 1966).

Braun & Schneider (eds), *Historic Costume in Pictures* (New York: Dover Publications Inc.,1975).

Cockburn, J.S. (ed.) *Crime in England 1550–1800* (London: Methuen & Co. Ltd., 1977).

Coupe, R., *Australian Bushrangers* (Sydney: New Holland, 1998).

Davitt, M., *Leaves From a Prison Diary* (Shannon: Irish University Press, 1972).

Fielding, H., *Jonathon Wild* (New York: The New American Library, 1743).

Fowler, W. and Sweeney, P., *The Illustrated Encyclopaedia of Pistols, Revolvers and Submachine Guns* (London: Hermes House, 2007).

Fowler, W. and Sweeney, P., *The World Encyclopaedia of Rifles and Machine Guns* (London: Hermes House, 2007).

Gardiner, S.R. (ed.), *The Constitutional Documents of the Puritan Revolution 1625 –1160* (Oxford: Oxford at the Clarendon Press, 1889).

Grose, C., *A Dictionary of the Vulgar Tongue* (Adelaide: Bibliophile Books, 1811).

Hibbert, C., *The Roots of Evil* (London: Weidenfeld & Nicolson, 1963).

Kyll, Thomas, *The Trial of the Notorious Highwayman Richard Turpin,* (London: Ward and Chandler Booksellers, 1739).

Lister, M., *Costume* (London: Barrie and Jenkins Ltd., 1967).

Low, D.A., *Thieves' Kitchen* (London: J.M. Dent & Sons Ltd., 1982).

Newgate, T.O., *The Newgate Calendar* (London).

Palmer, R. (ed.), *Everyman's book of British Ballads* (London: J.M. Dent & Sons Ltd., 1980).

Pottle, F.A. (ed.), *Boswell's London Journal* (London: The Harborough Publishing Co., Ltd., 1950).

Turberville, A.S. (ed.), *Johnson's England* (Oxford: Clarendon Press, 1933).

Whibley, C., *A Book of Scoundrels*.

Wilkinson, F., *Arms and Armour* (London: Hamlyn Publishing Group, 1971).

Zirker, M.R. (ed.), *Henry Fielding: An Enquiry into the Causes of the Late Increase of Robbers and Related Writings* (Oxford: Clarendon Press, 1988).

INDEX